BIG LEFT HANDED GUITAR CHORD BOOK

By Richard Moran

6 Strings - Big Left Handed Guitar Chord Book

Edition I

www.MoranEducation.com/6Strings

ISBN 978-1-4716-5376-6

Introduction

Our Guitar Chord Grids explained

6 Strings employs a unique horizontal grid layout to display our guitar chords. This is a system proven to speed up the learning process, as it is far easier to absorb the information in this format rather than in the vertical format usually employed in guitar books.

The circles shown on our guitar chord diagrams each correspond to a finger on the right hand.

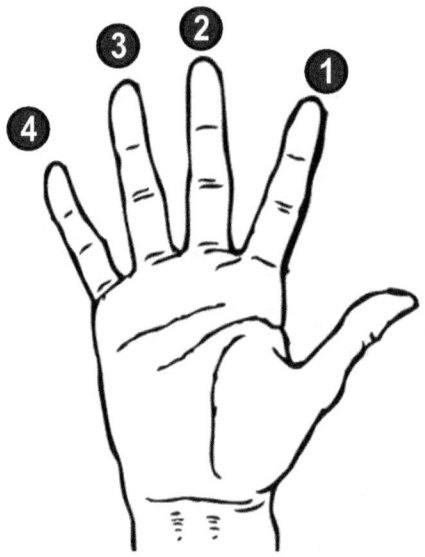

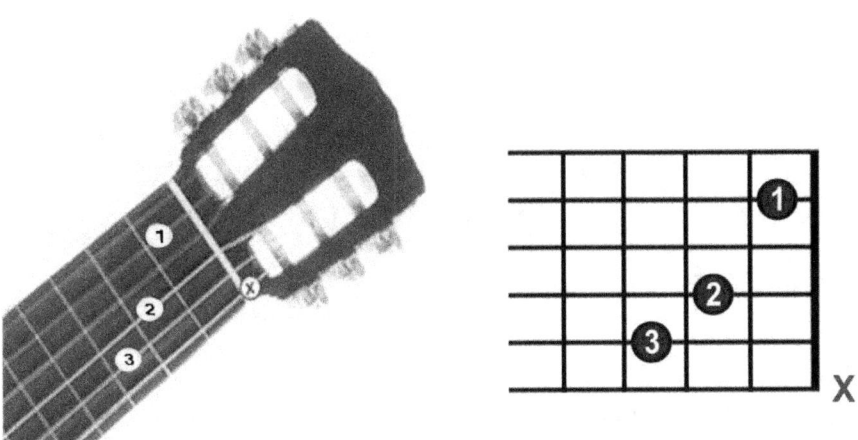

For example, to play this chord of C Major, put fingers one two and three in the positions indicated, and either do not play the lowest string, or deaden the string by touching it lightly with either the adjacent third finger, or with the fourth finger.

Next to the grid on the right, you can see how this would actually look on the guitar shown on the left.

An 'X' to the right of a string shows that the string should not be played or strummed, or should be deadened by another finger.

In this book, the top line of the grid or chord diagram always corresponds to the highest sounding string on the guitar. The lowest line corresponds to the lowest sounding (and thickest) string.

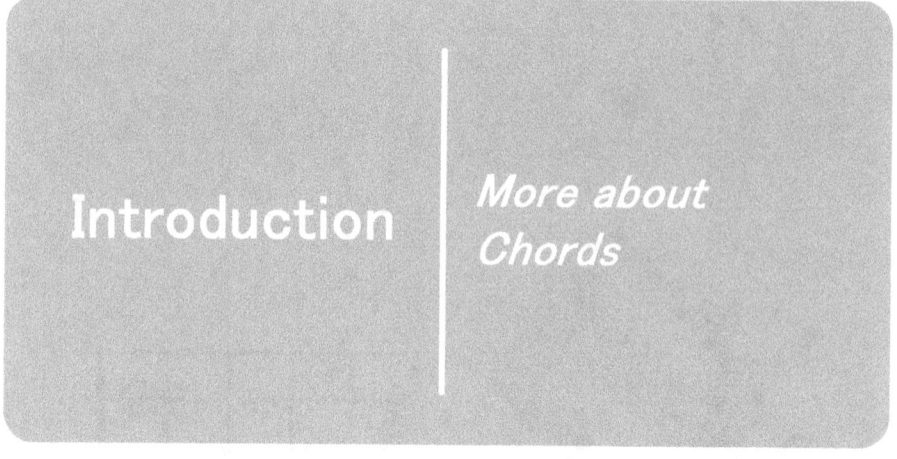

Introduction | *More about Chords*

Bar Chords, and chords in higher positions:

Here's an alternative fingering for the chord of C Major. To play the chord, '8 fr.' means you must move your right hand up to the eighth fret of the guitar. You'll notice that there are multiple notes to be played with the first finger. This is called a Bar. Place the first finger flat across all six strings on the eighth fret, and place fingers two three and four as normal to create the chord.

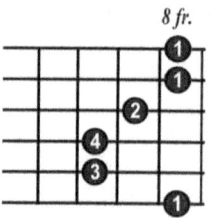

Chords where no fret number is specified always start at the first fret.

Quick tips:

Is your chord not listed in the book? Remember that...

    A ♭ can also be written as G#
    B ♭ can also be written as A#
    C# can also be written as D ♭
    E ♭ can also be written as D#
    F# can also be written as G ♭

... so if the given chord is D ♭ maj7, substitute C#maj7 instead.. it's actually exactly the same chord!

Other chord naming conventions:

There are multiple naming conventions for chords. We've used the most popular versions in our book. In case you encounter any other ways of writing these chords, we've put together a quick guide below...

In these examples, we've substituted 'X' for the first letter of the chord.

Major Chords - These are sometimes written as XMaj, or XM. In this book, we use just 'X'

Minor Chords - Are sometimes written as Xmin or Xmi. We use Xm.

Chords with a '-' sign in them are also sometimes written with a ' ♭ ' instead

Chords with a '+' sign in them are also sometimes written with a '#' instead

Diminished Seventh Chords are shown as a 'X°'. They can also be written as X°7, Xdim7, X-7, and Xdim

Suspended Chords - 'sus' chords can also be written as 'sus4'

'7sus', 'sus7', and '7sus4' are all exactly the same.

Augmented chords can be written as '+', '#5', '+5', or 'aug'

Major Sixth chords can be written as '6', 'Maj6, or 'M6'

Major Sixth add Nine can be written as '6/9, 6(add9'), 'Maj6(add9)', or 'M6(add9)'

'X7' is sometimes written as 'X Dom 7'

A♭

A♭ is also known as G#

Chords

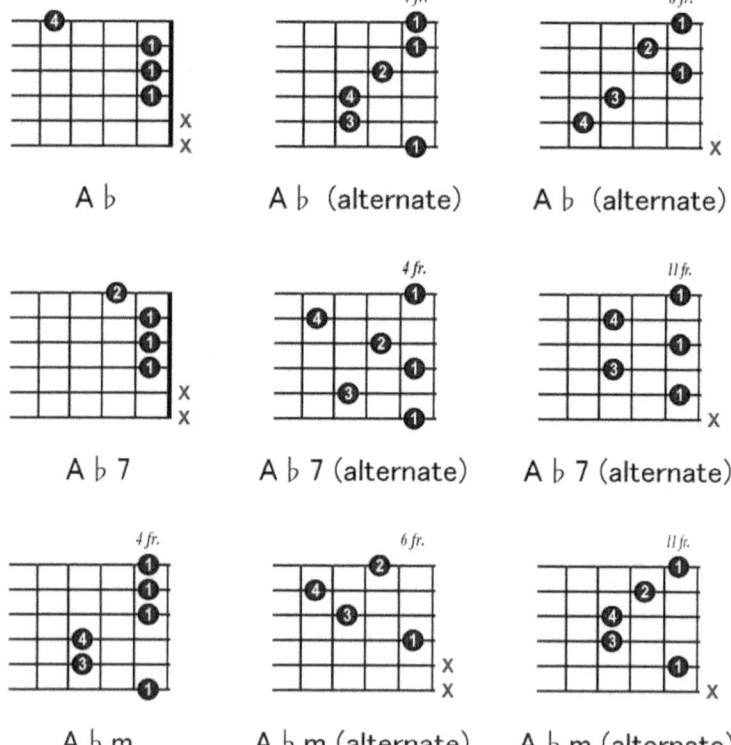

A♭   A♭ (alternate)   A♭ (alternate)

A♭7   A♭7 (alternate)   A♭7 (alternate)

A♭m   A♭m (alternate)   A♭m (alternate)

Big Left Handed Guitar Chord Book
©2012 Moran Education http://www.MoranEducation.com/6Strings

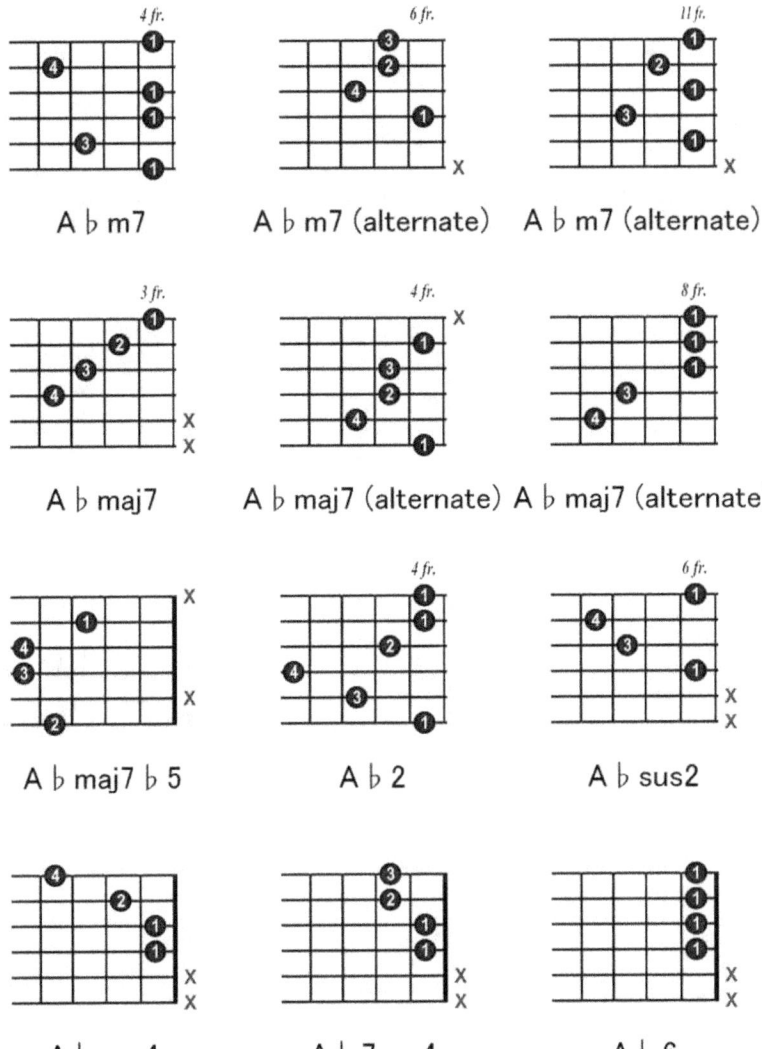

A♭ m7 A♭ m7 (alternate) A♭ m7 (alternate)

A♭ maj7 A♭ maj7 (alternate) A♭ maj7 (alternate)

A♭ maj7♭5 A♭ 2 A♭ sus2

A♭ sus4 A♭ 7sus4 A♭ 6

A♭ Chords | *Continued*

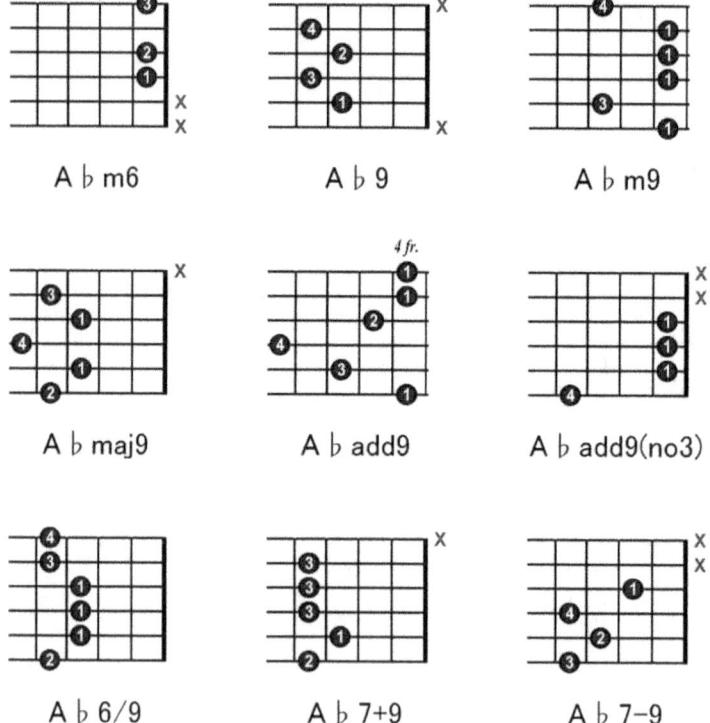

A♭ m6

A♭ 9

4 fr.
A♭ m9

A♭ maj9

4 fr.
A♭ add9

A♭ add9(no3)

A♭ 6/9

A♭ 7+9

A♭ 7−9

A♭

Big Left Handed Guitar Chord Book
©2012 Moran Education http://www.MoranEducation.com/6Strings

8

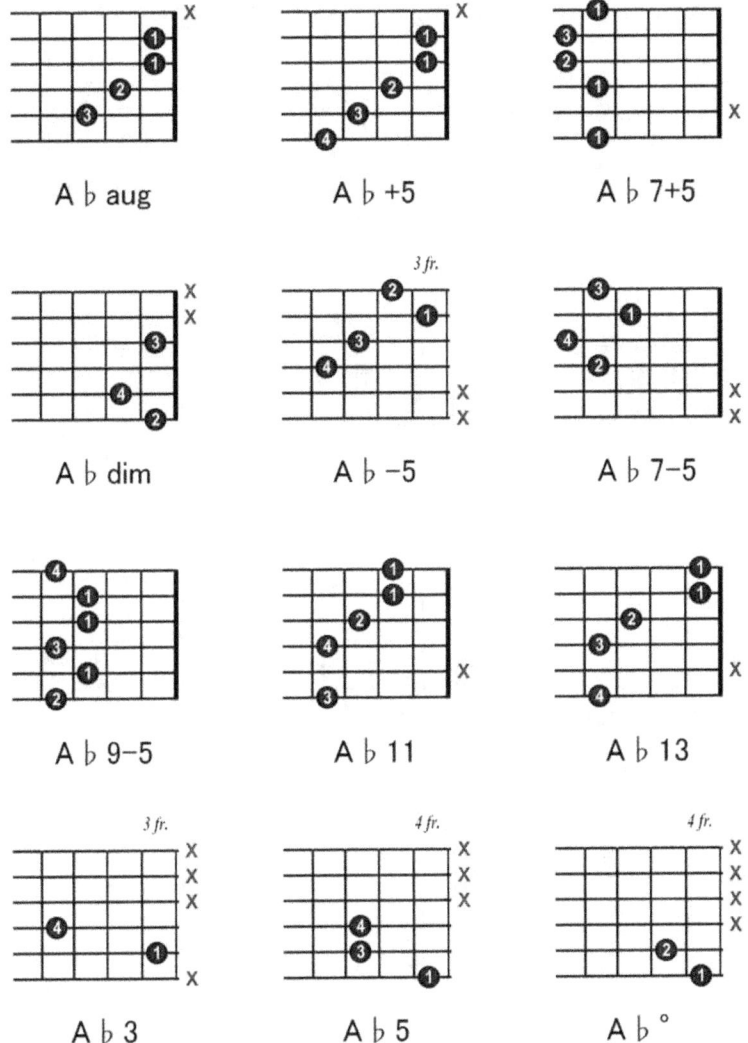

A♭ aug

A♭ +5

A♭ 7+5

A♭ dim

A♭ −5

A♭ 7−5

A♭ 9−5

A♭ 11

A♭ 13

A♭ 3
Power Chord

A♭ 5
Power Chord

A♭ °
Power Chord

A

Chords

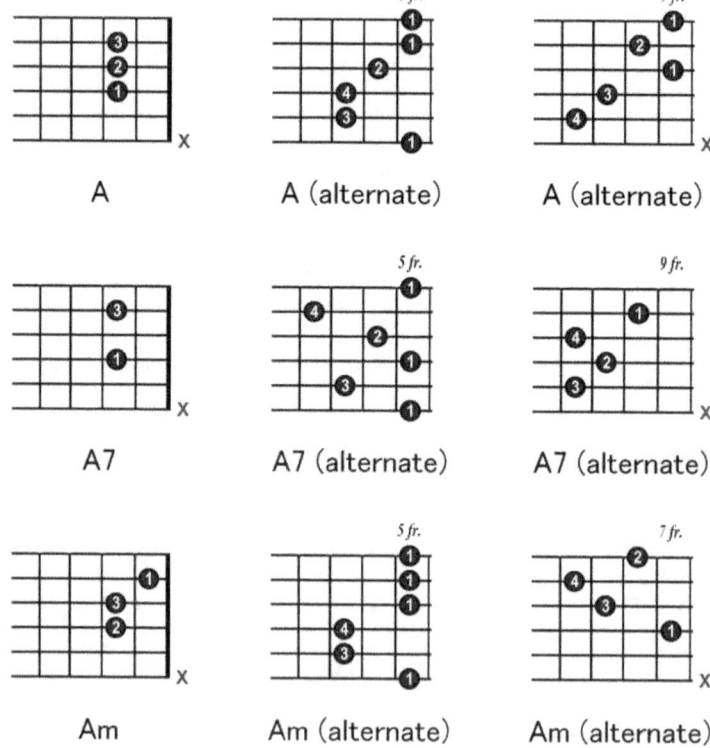

A

A (alternate) — 5 fr.

A (alternate) — 9 fr.

A7

A7 (alternate) — 5 fr.

A7 (alternate) — 9 fr.

Am

Am (alternate) — 5 fr.

Am (alternate) — 7 fr.

Big Left Handed Guitar Chord Book
©2012 Moran Education http://www.MoranEducation.com/6Strings

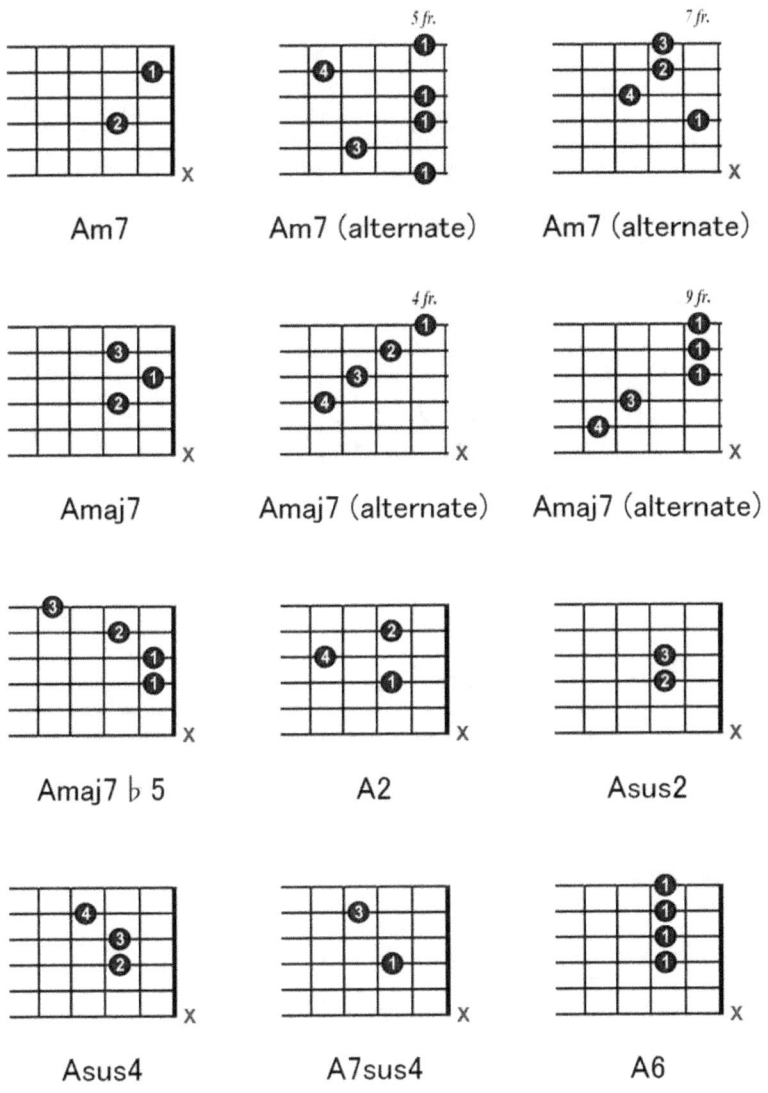

Am7

Am7 (alternate)

Am7 (alternate)

Amaj7

Amaj7 (alternate)

Amaj7 (alternate)

Amaj7 ♭ 5

A2

Asus2

Asus4

A7sus4

A6

A
Chords

Continued

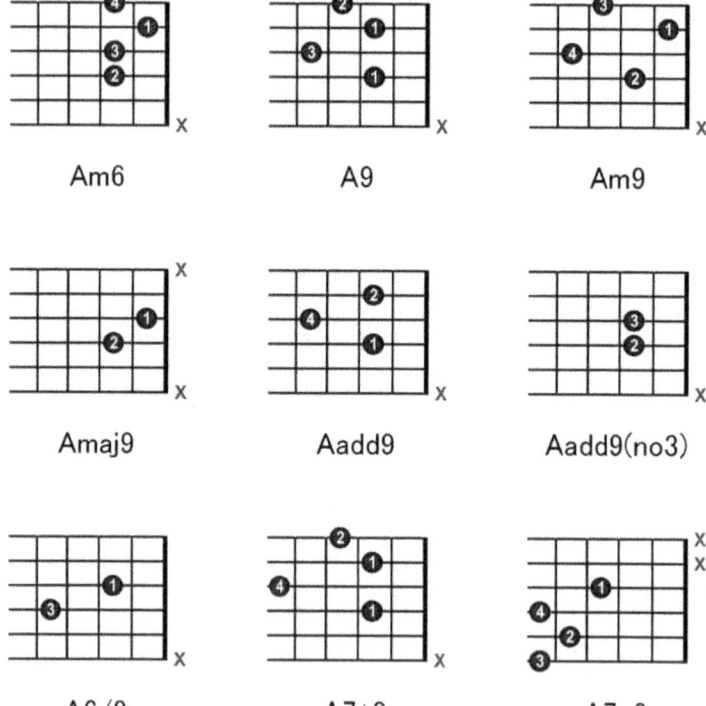

Am6

A9

Am9

Amaj9

Aadd9

Aadd9(no3)

A6/9

A7+9

A7−9

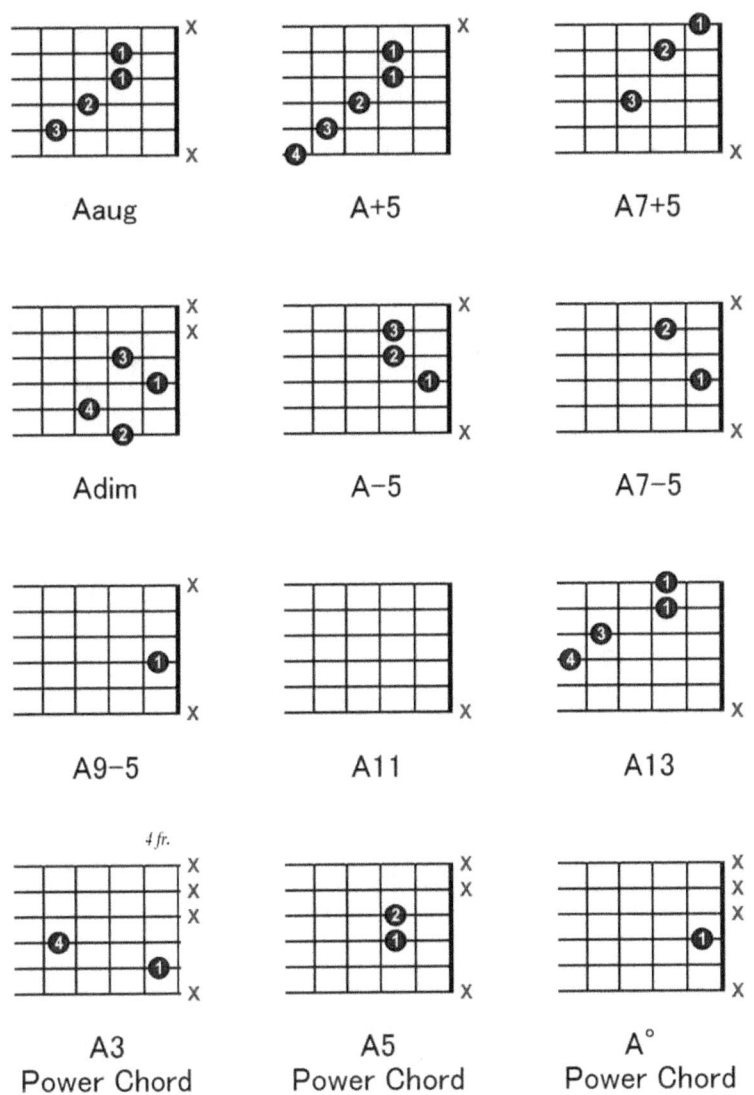

Aaug A+5 A7+5

Adim A−5 A7−5

A9−5 A11 A13

4 fr.

A3
Power Chord

A5
Power Chord

A°
Power Chord

B♭
Chords

B♭ is also known as A#

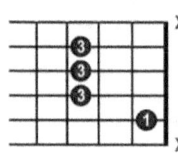

B♭

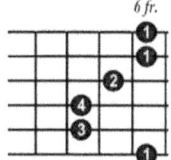

B♭ (alternate)

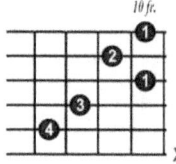

B♭ (alternate)

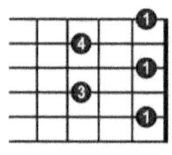

B♭7

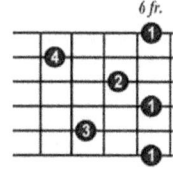

B♭7 (alternate)

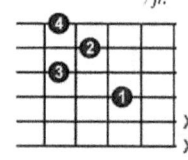

B♭7 (alternate)

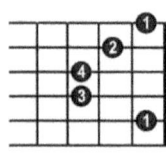

B♭m

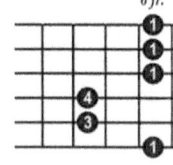

B♭m (alternate)

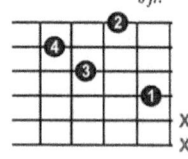

B♭m (alternate)

B♭

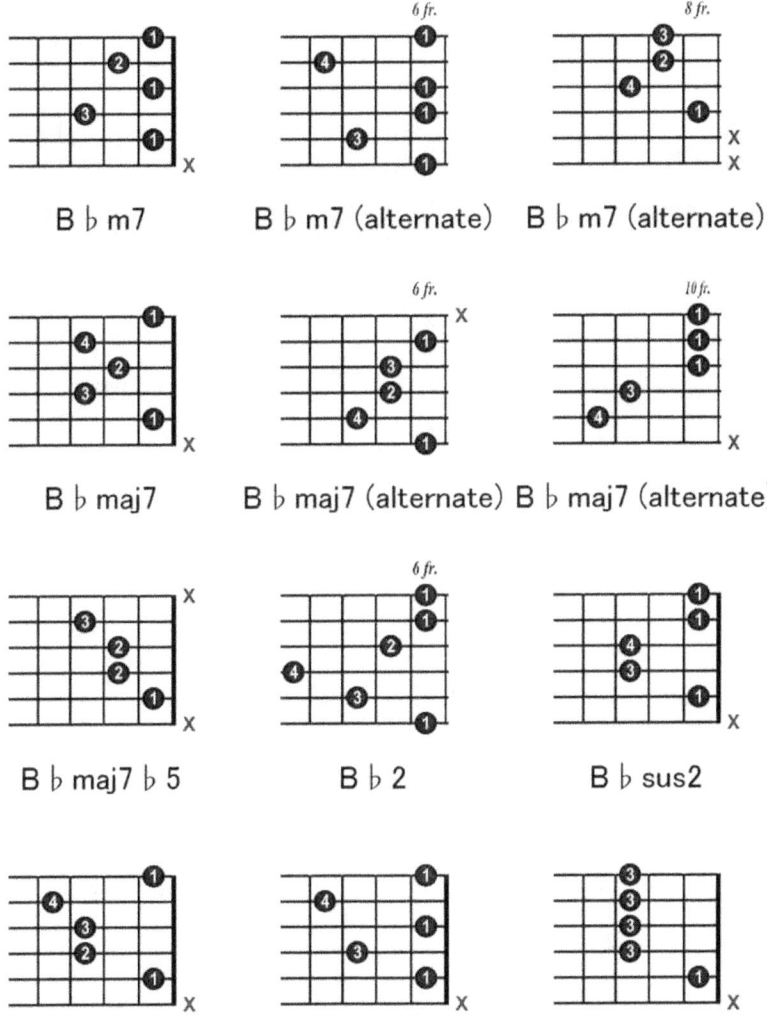

B♭m7 — B♭m7 (alternate) *6 fr.* — B♭m7 (alternate) *8 fr.*

B♭maj7 — B♭maj7 (alternate) *6 fr.* — B♭maj7 (alternate) *10 fr.*

B♭maj7♭5 — B♭2 *6 fr.* — B♭sus2

B♭sus4 — B♭7sus4 — B♭6

B♭

Chords

Continued

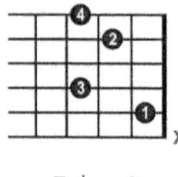

B ♭ m6

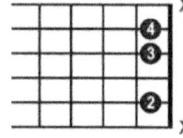

B ♭ 9

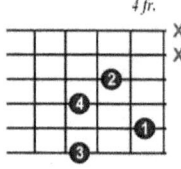

B ♭ m9

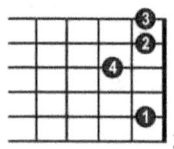

B ♭ maj9

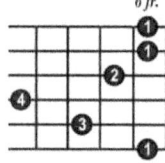

B ♭ add9

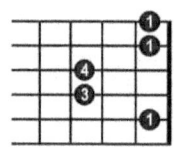

B ♭ add9(no3)

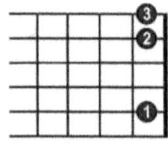

B ♭ 6/9

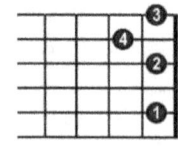

B ♭ 7+9

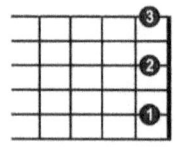

B ♭ 7−9

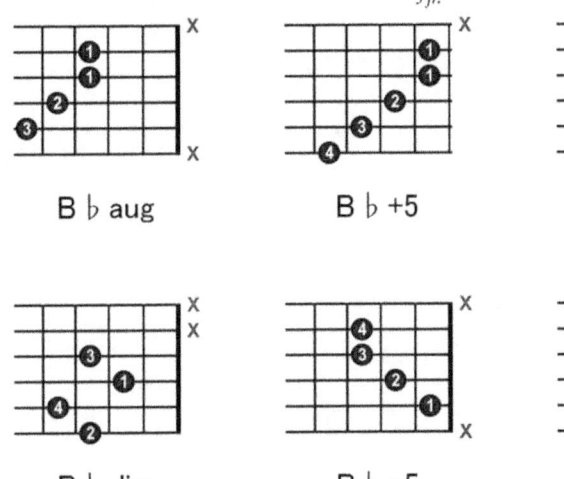

3 fr.

B♭ aug   B♭ +5   B♭ 7+5

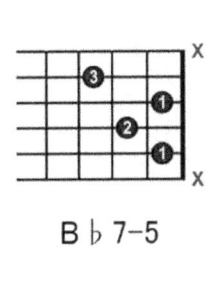

B♭ dim   B♭ –5   B♭ 7–5

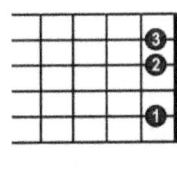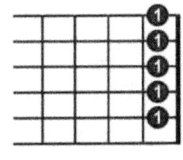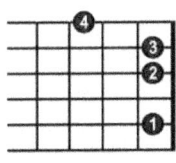

B♭ 9–5   B♭ 11   B♭ 13

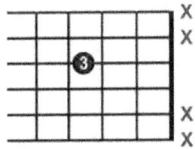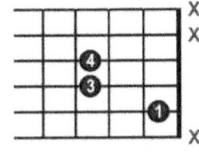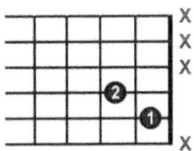

B♭ 3   B♭ 5   B♭ °
Power Chord   Power Chord   Power Chord

B

Chords

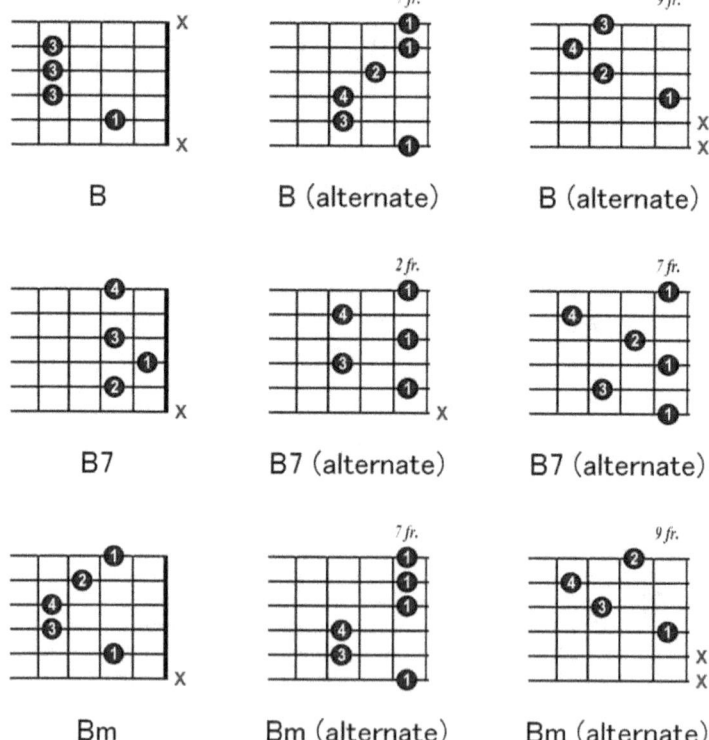

B

B (alternate) — 7 fr.

B (alternate) — 9 fr.

B7

B7 (alternate) — 2 fr.

B7 (alternate) — 7 fr.

Bm

Bm (alternate) — 7 fr.

Bm (alternate) — 9 fr.

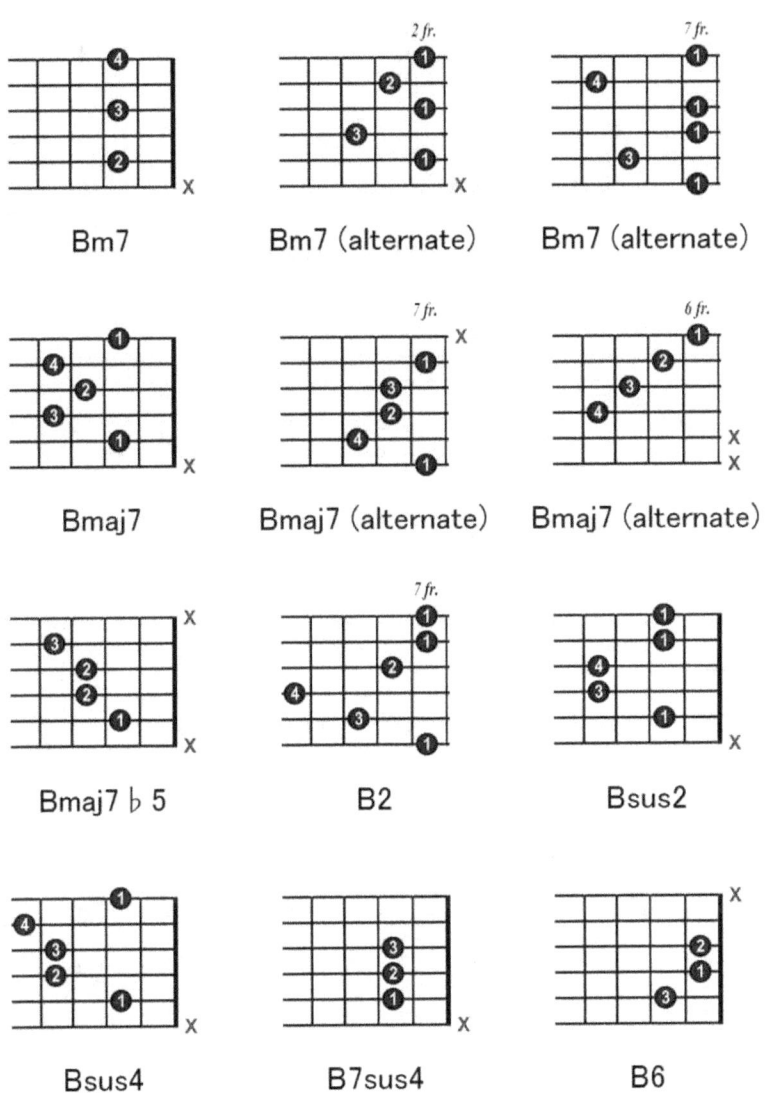

Bm7

Bm7 (alternate)

Bm7 (alternate)

Bmaj7

Bmaj7 (alternate)

Bmaj7 (alternate)

Bmaj7 ♭ 5

B2

Bsus2

Bsus4

B7sus4

B6

B

Continued

Chords

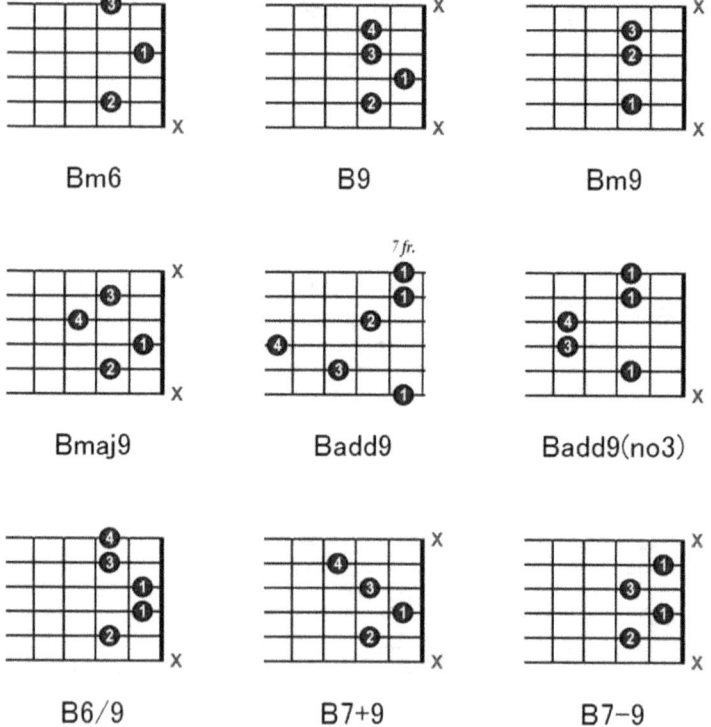

Bm6

B9

Bm9

Bmaj9

Badd9

Badd9(no3)

B6/9

B7+9

B7−9

Big Left Handed Guitar Chord Book

©2012 Moran Education http://www.MoranEducation.com/6Strings

B

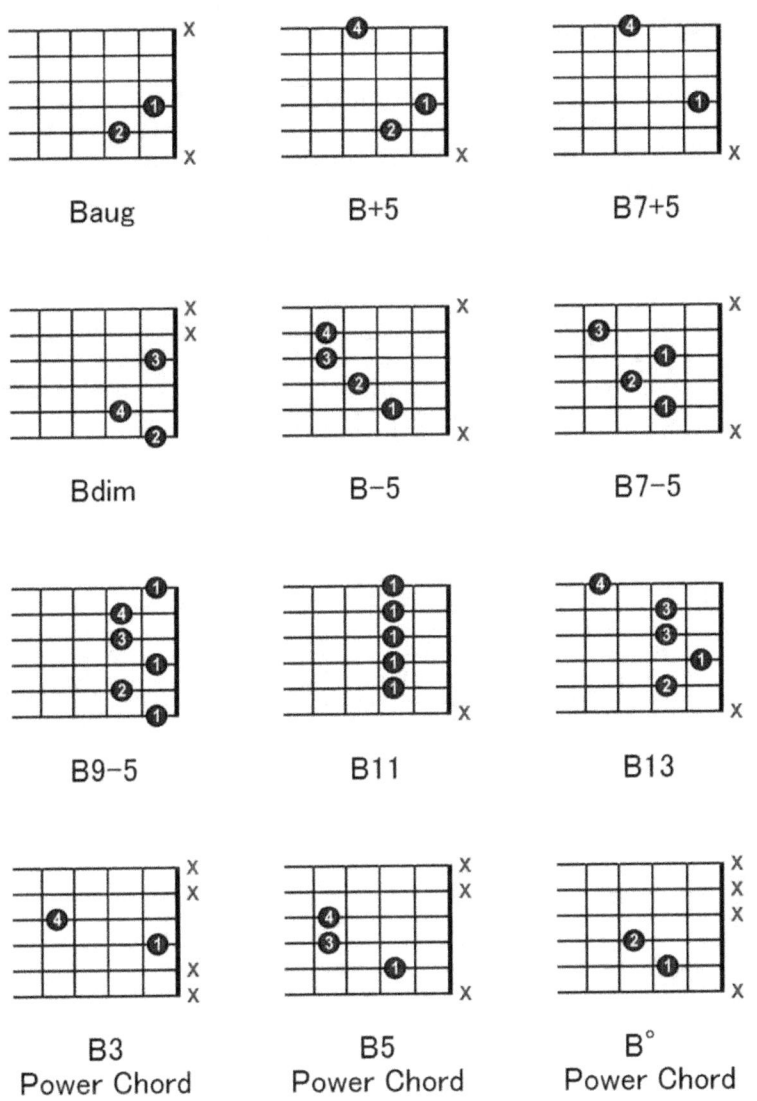

Baug

B+5

B7+5

Bdim

B−5

B7−5

B9−5

B11

B13

B3
Power Chord

B5
Power Chord

B°
Power Chord

C

Chords

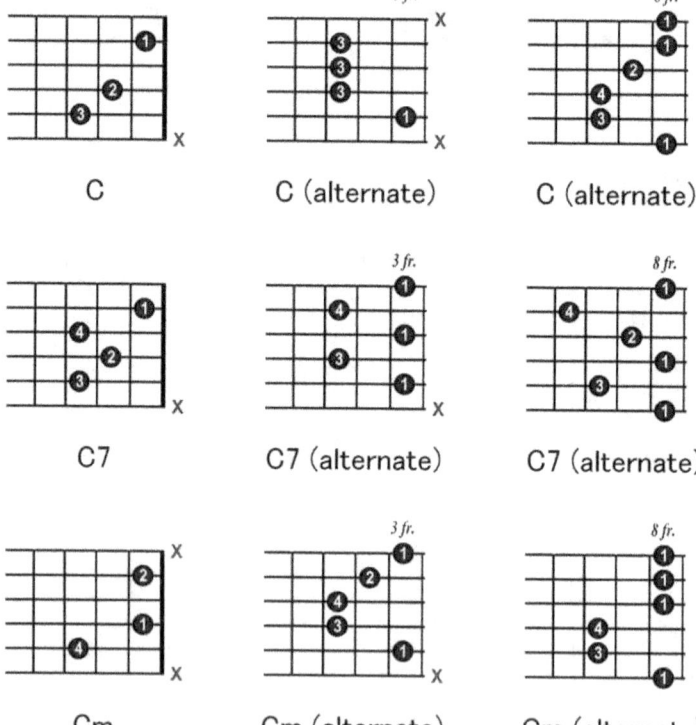

C

C (alternate) — 3 fr.

C (alternate) — 8 fr.

C7

C7 (alternate) — 3 fr.

C7 (alternate) — 8 fr.

Cm

Cm (alternate) — 3 fr.

Cm (alternate) — 8 fr.

Big Left Handed Guitar Chord Book
©2012 Moran Education http://www.MoranEducation.com/6Strings

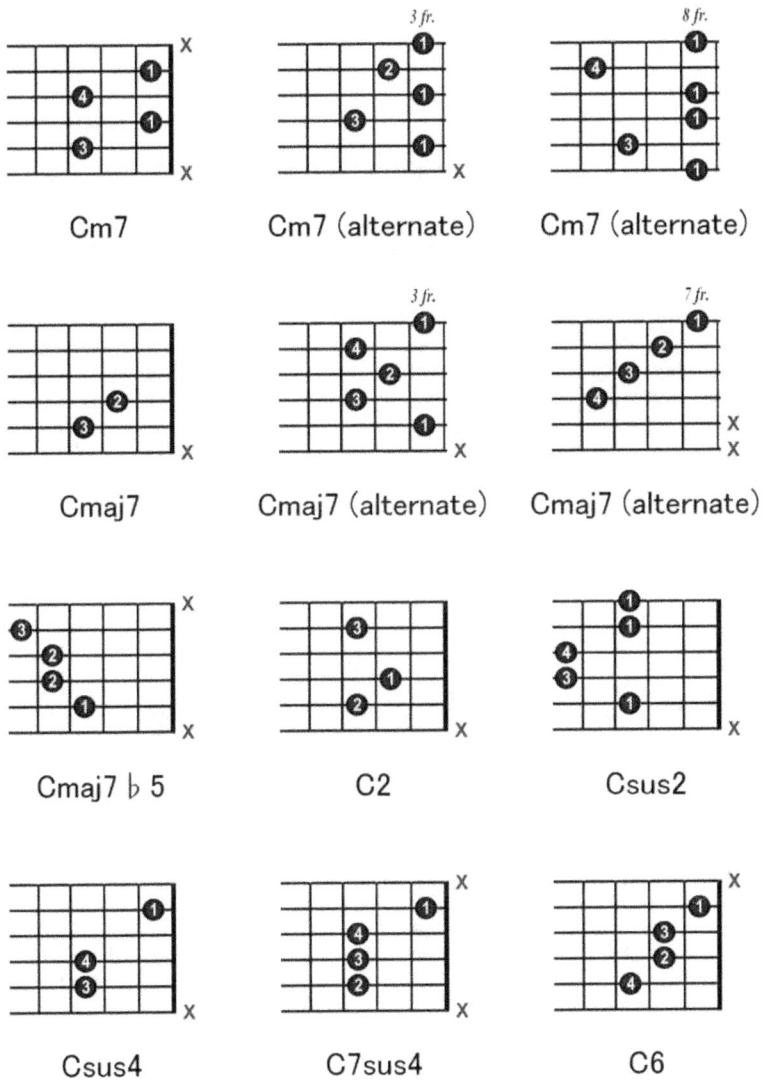

C

Cm7

Cm7 (alternate)

Cm7 (alternate)

Cmaj7

Cmaj7 (alternate)

Cmaj7 (alternate)

Cmaj7 ♭ 5

C2

Csus2

Csus4

C7sus4

C6

C Chords

Continued

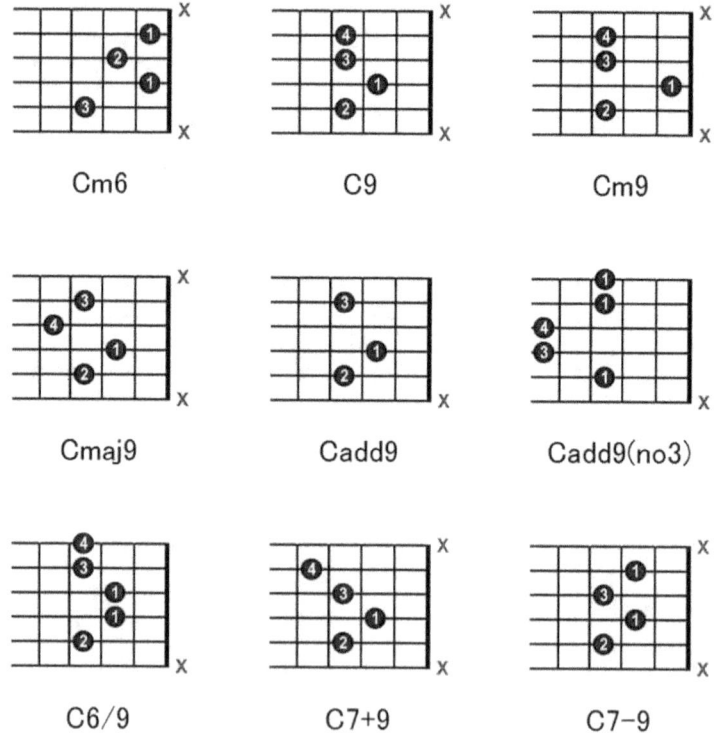

Cm6	C9	Cm9
Cmaj9	Cadd9	Cadd9(no3)
C6/9	C7+9	C7−9

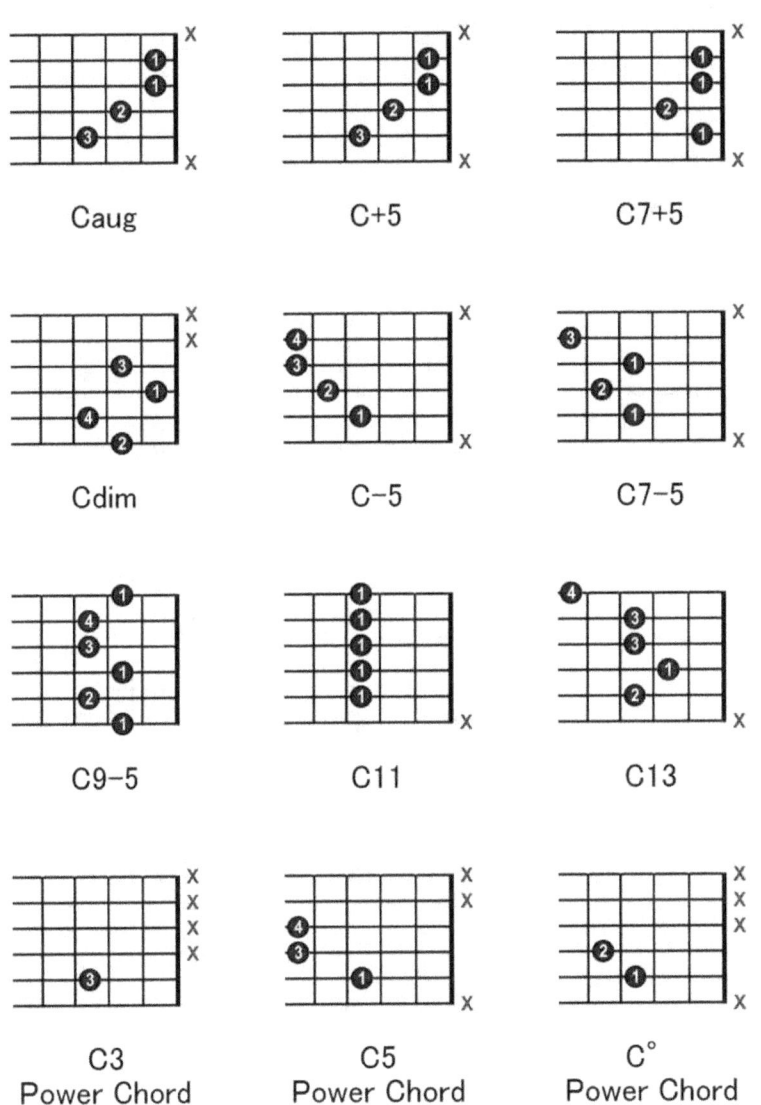

Caug

C+5

C7+5

Cdim

C-5

C7-5

C9-5

C11

C13

C3
Power Chord

C5
Power Chord

C°
Power Chord

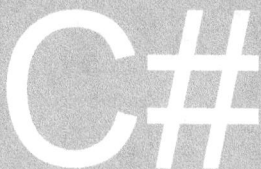

C#

C# is also known as D♭

Chords

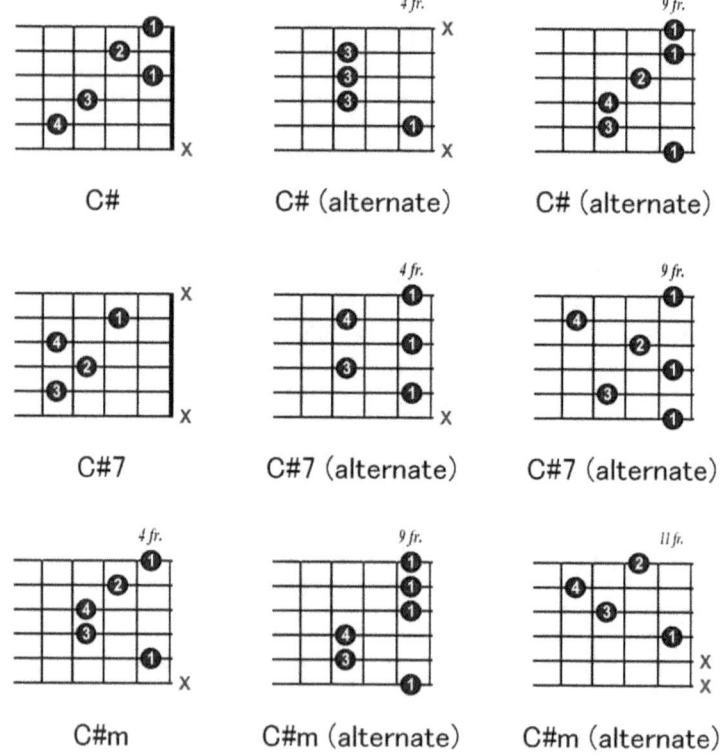

C#

C# (alternate)   4 fr.

C# (alternate)   9 fr.

C#7

C#7 (alternate)   4 fr.

C#7 (alternate)   9 fr.

C#m   4 fr.

C#m (alternate)   9 fr.

C#m (alternate)   11 fr.

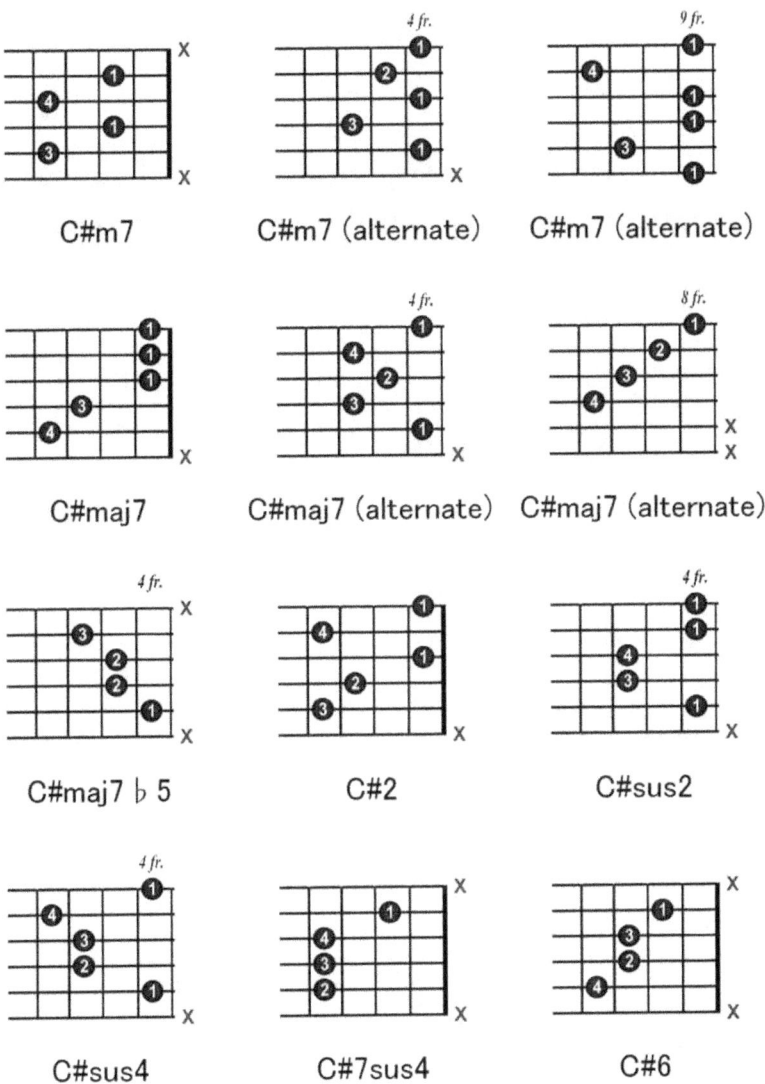

C#m7 C#m7 (alternate) C#m7 (alternate)

C#maj7 C#maj7 (alternate) C#maj7 (alternate)

C#maj7 ♭ 5 C#2 C#sus2

C#sus4 C#7sus4 C#6

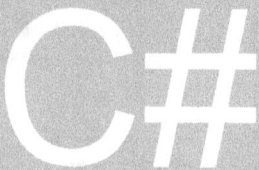

C# Continued

Chords

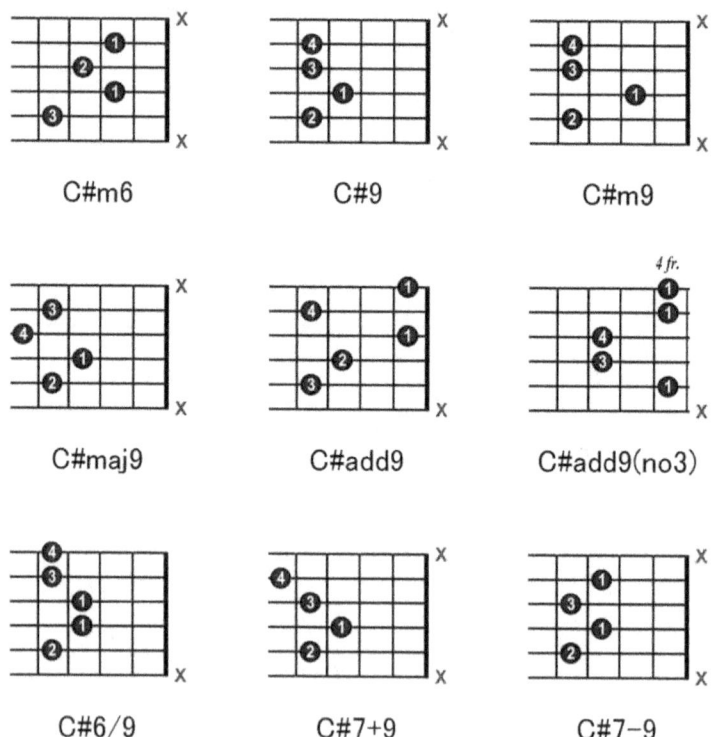

C#m6	C#9	C#m9

C#maj9	C#add9	C#add9(no3)

C#6/9	C#7+9	C#7−9

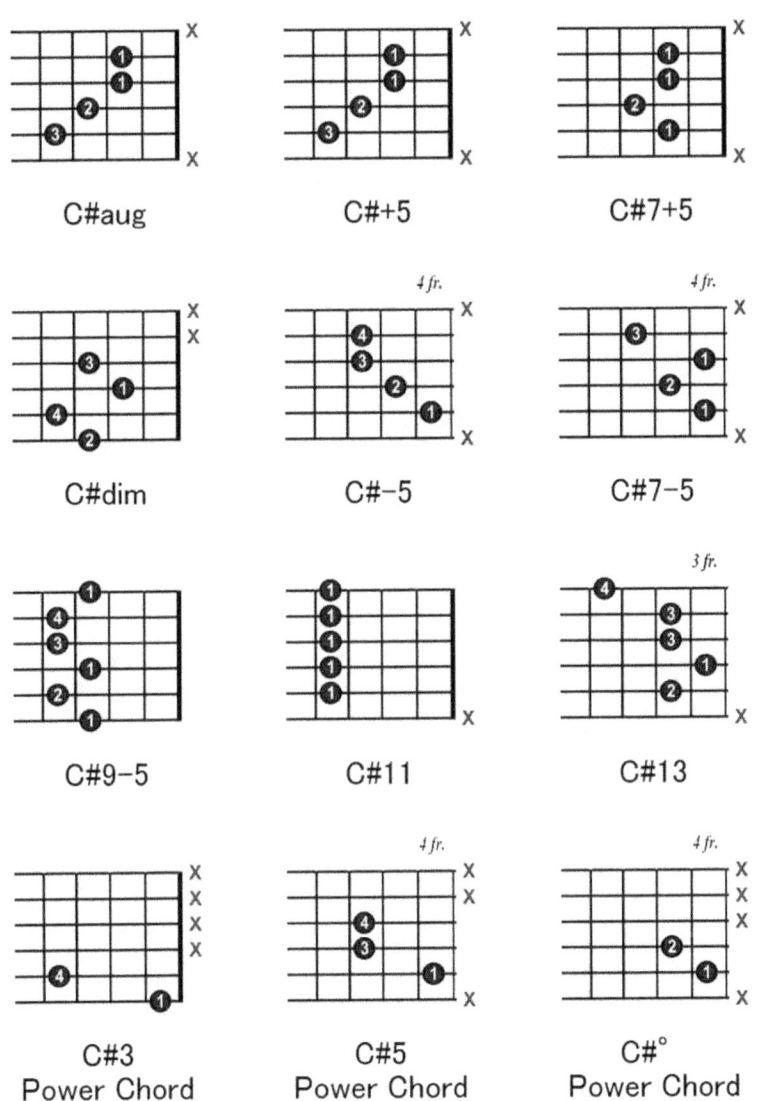

C#aug

C#+5

C#7+5

C#dim

C#−5

C#7−5

C#9−5

C#11

C#13

C#3
Power Chord

C#5
Power Chord

C#°
Power Chord

D

Chords

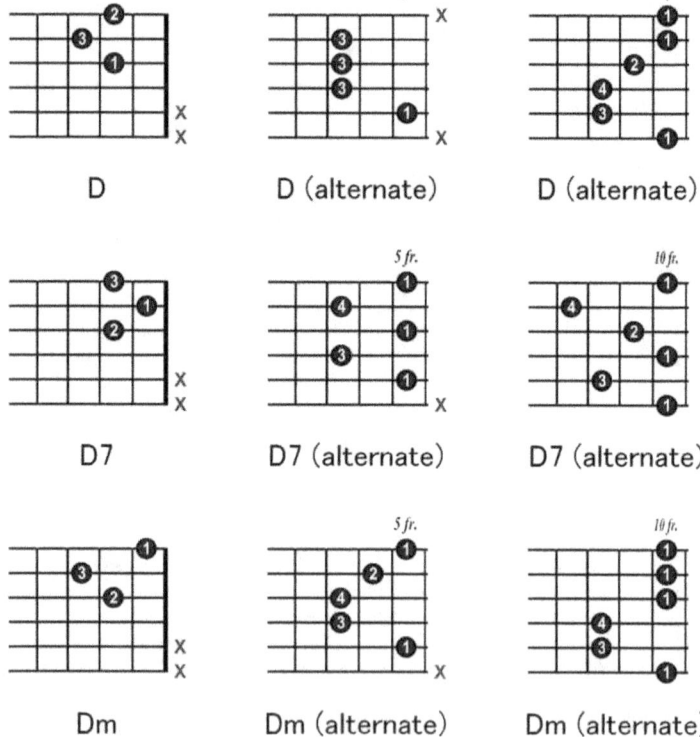

D   D (alternate)   D (alternate)

D7   D7 (alternate)   D7 (alternate)

Dm   Dm (alternate)   Dm (alternate)

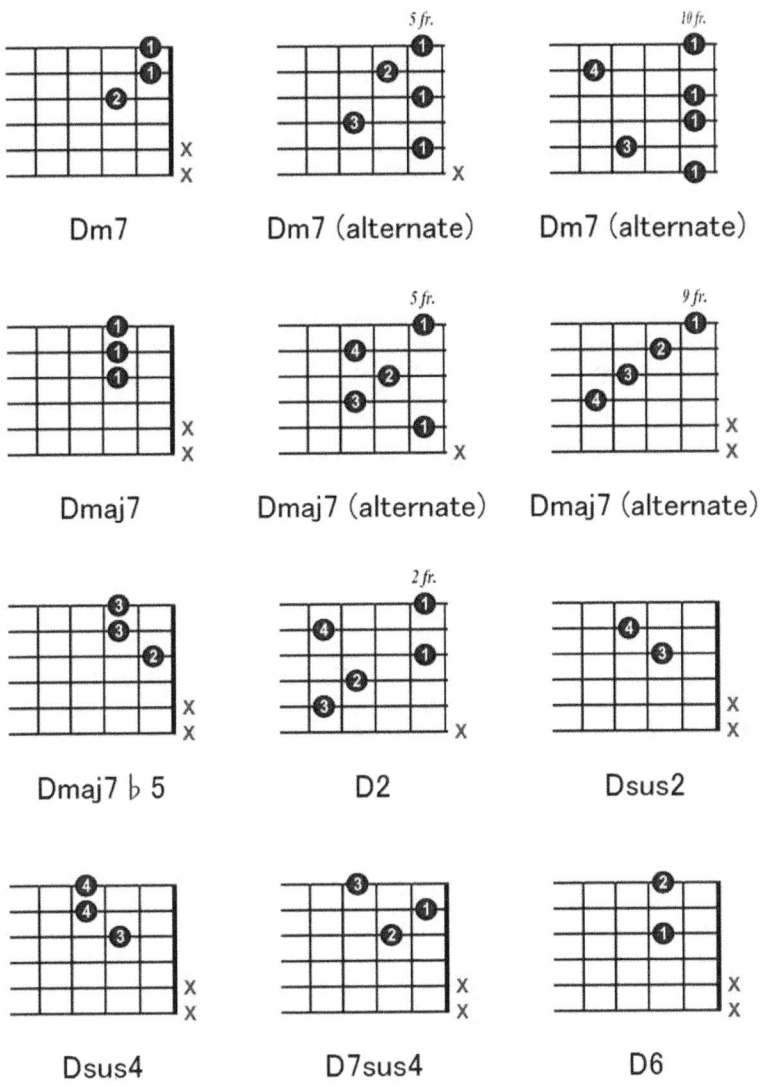

Dm7   Dm7 (alternate)   Dm7 (alternate)

Dmaj7   Dmaj7 (alternate)   Dmaj7 (alternate)

Dmaj7 ♭ 5   D2   Dsus2

Dsus4   D7sus4   D6

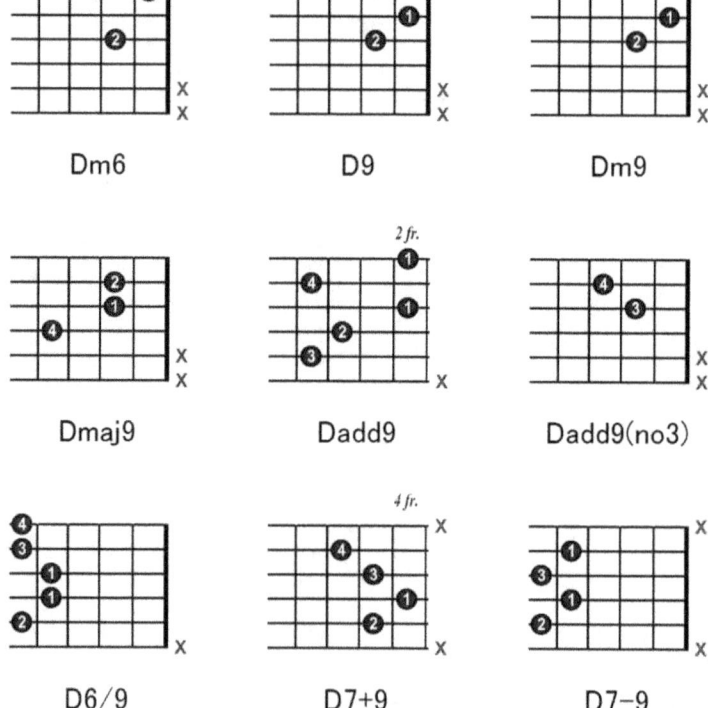

Dm6   D9   Dm9

Dmaj9   Dadd9   Dadd9(no3)

D6/9   D7+9   D7−9

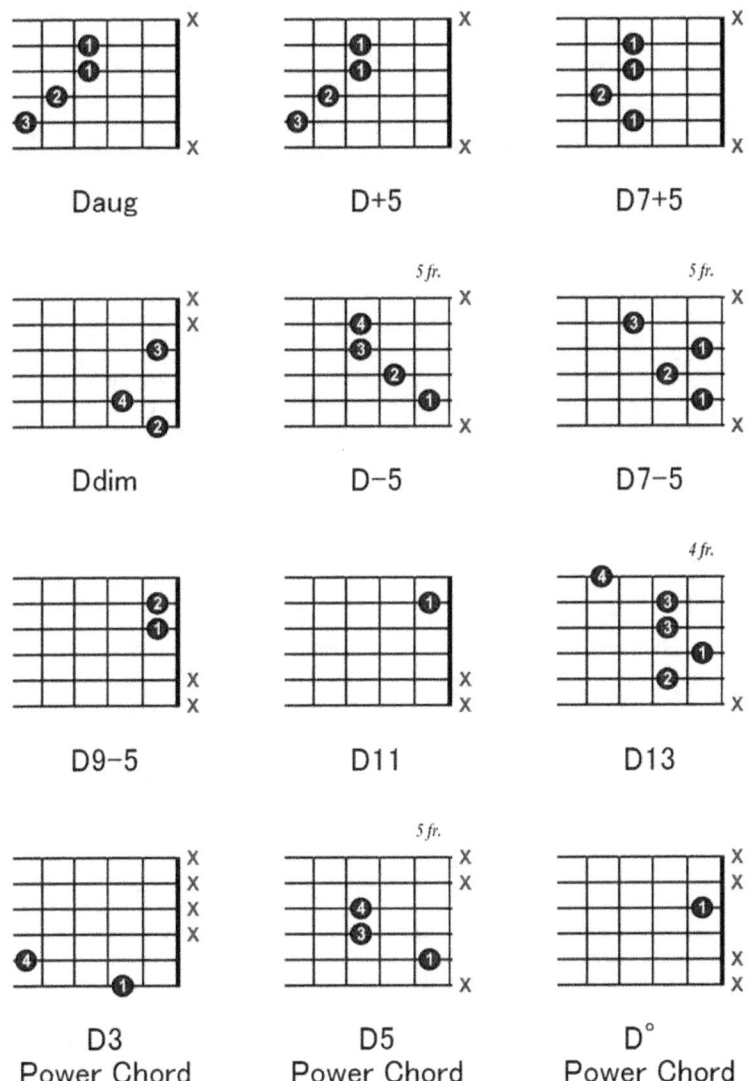

Daug

D+5

D7+5

Ddim

D−5

D7−5

D9−5

D11

D13

D3
Power Chord

D5
Power Chord

D°
Power Chord

E♭

E ♭ is also known as D#

Chords

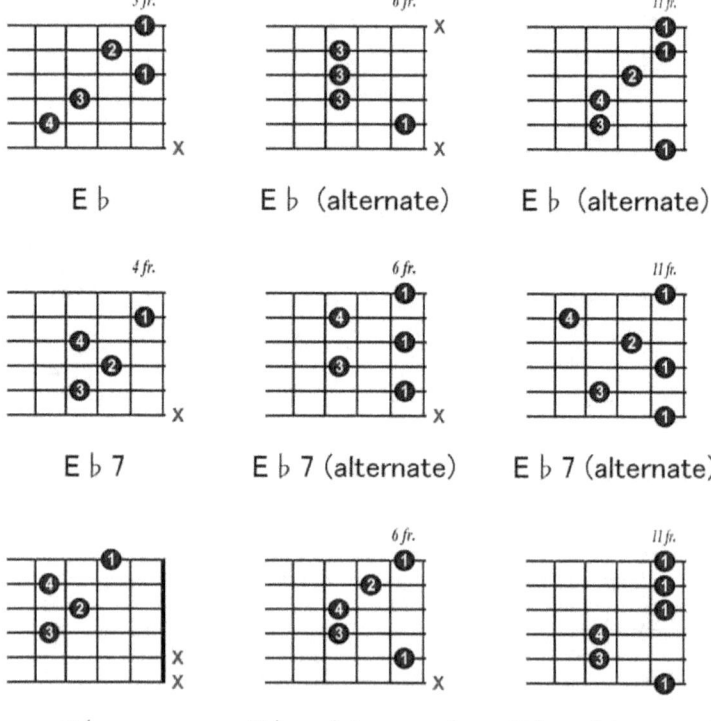

E ♭

E ♭ (alternate)

E ♭ (alternate)

E ♭ 7

E ♭ 7 (alternate)

E ♭ 7 (alternate)

E ♭ m

E ♭ m (alternate)

E ♭ m (alternate)

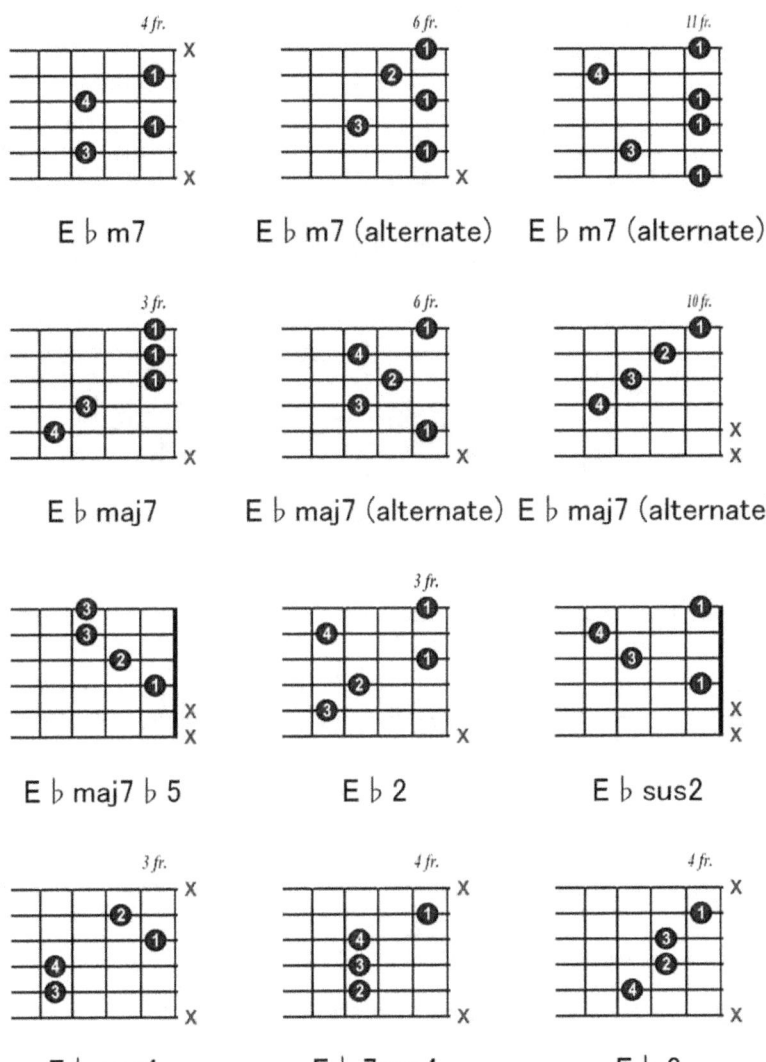

E♭ m7   E♭ m7 (alternate)   E♭ m7 (alternate)

E♭ maj7   E♭ maj7 (alternate)   E♭ maj7 (alternate)

E♭ maj7♭5   E♭ 2   E♭ sus2

E♭ sus4   E♭ 7sus4   E♭ 6

E♭

Chords

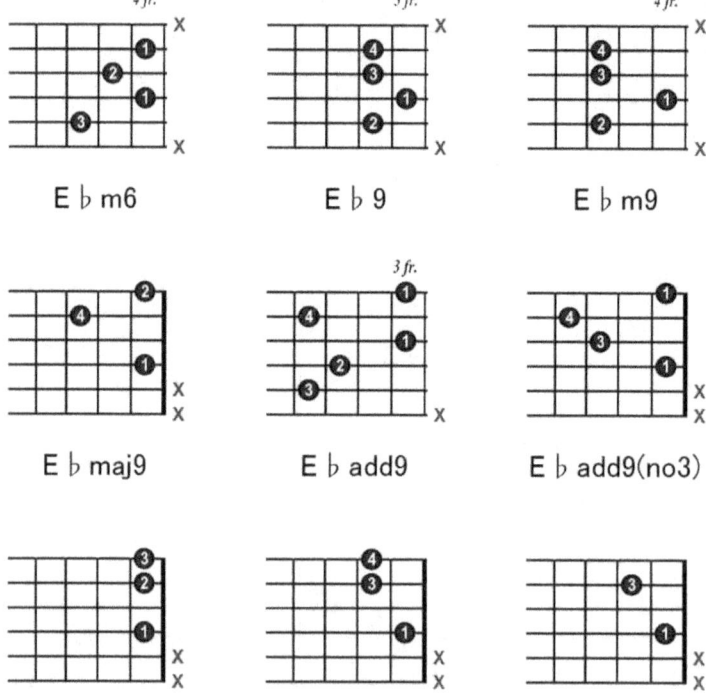

E♭ m6

E♭ 9

E♭ m9

E♭ maj9

E♭ add9

E♭ add9(no3)

E♭ 6/9

E♭ 7+9

E♭ 7−9

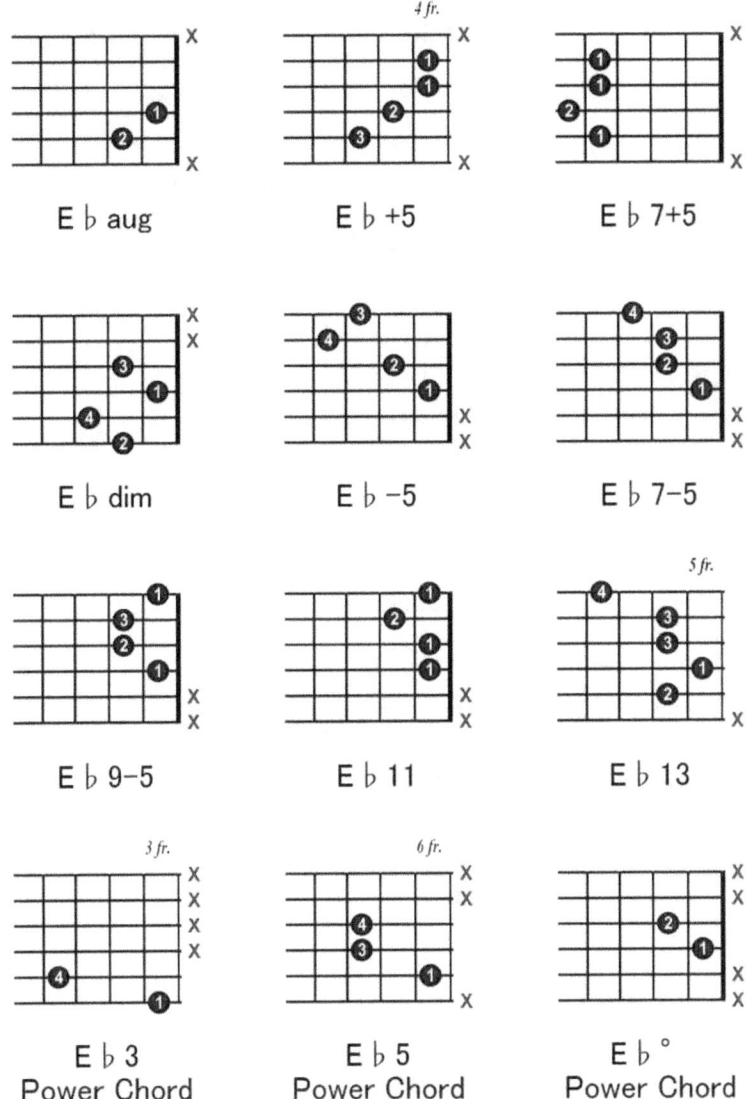

E ♭ aug

E ♭ +5

E ♭ 7+5

E ♭ dim

E ♭ −5

E ♭ 7−5

E ♭ 9−5

E ♭ 11

E ♭ 13

E ♭ 3
Power Chord

E ♭ 5
Power Chord

E ♭ °
Power Chord

E

Chords

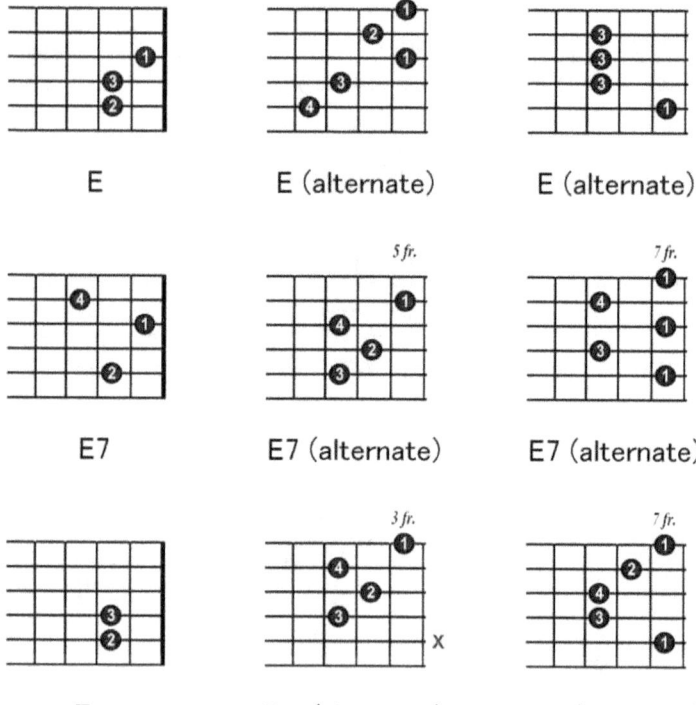

E   E (alternate) *4 fr.*   E (alternate) *7 fr.*

E7   E7 (alternate) *5 fr.*   E7 (alternate) *7 fr.*

Em   Em (alternate) *3 fr.*   Em (alternate) *7 fr.*

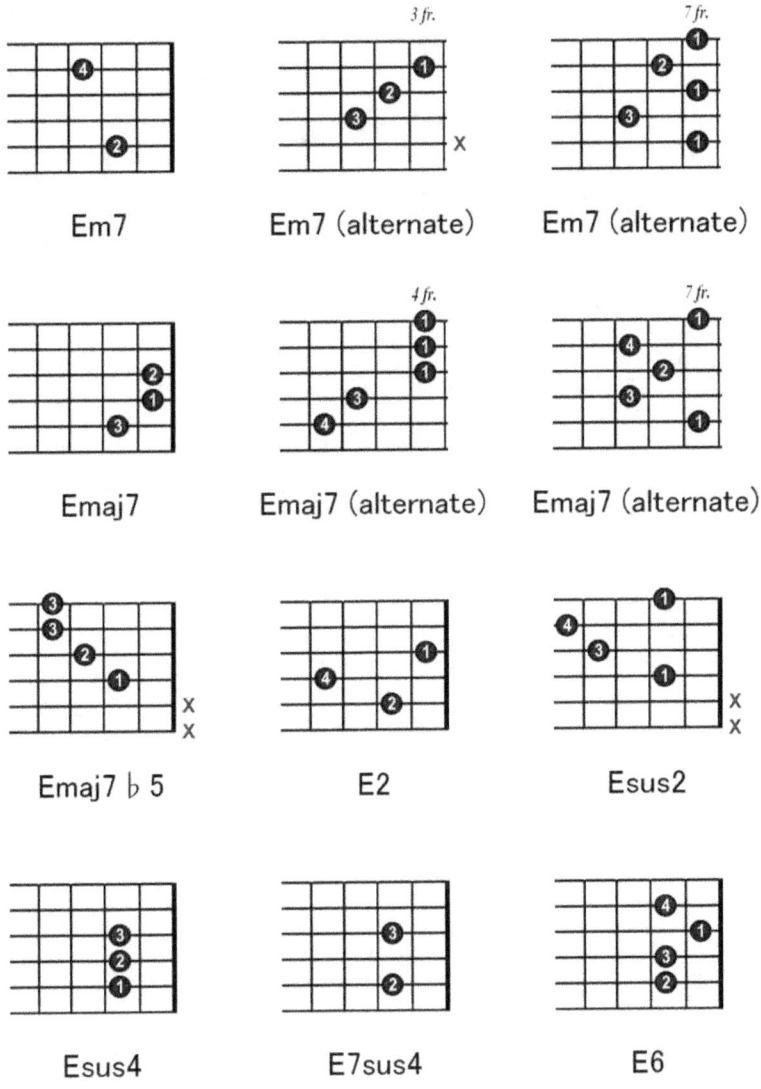

Em7   Em7 (alternate)   Em7 (alternate)

Emaj7   Emaj7 (alternate)   Emaj7 (alternate)

Emaj7 ♭ 5   E2   Esus2

Esus4   E7sus4   E6

E

Chivords

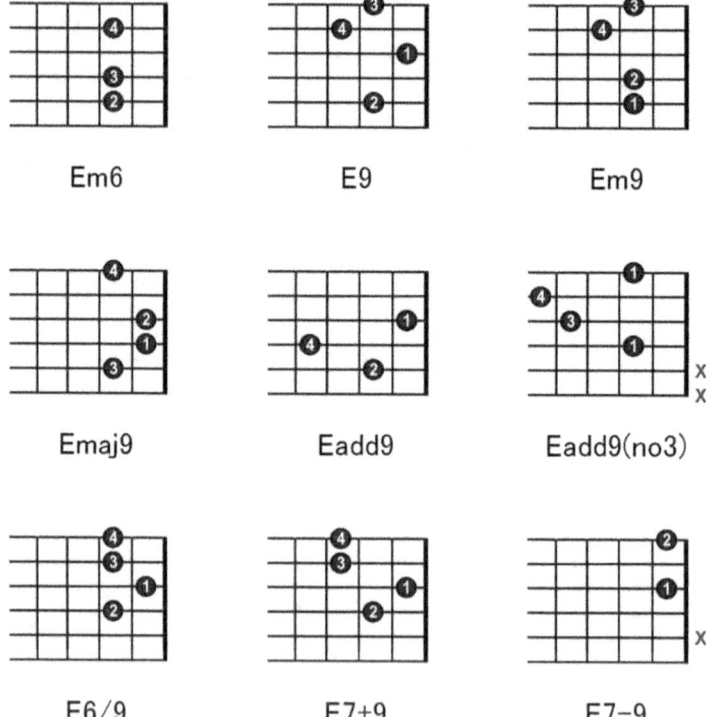

Em6   E9   Em9

Emaj9   Eadd9   Eadd9(no3)

E6/9   E7+9   E7-9

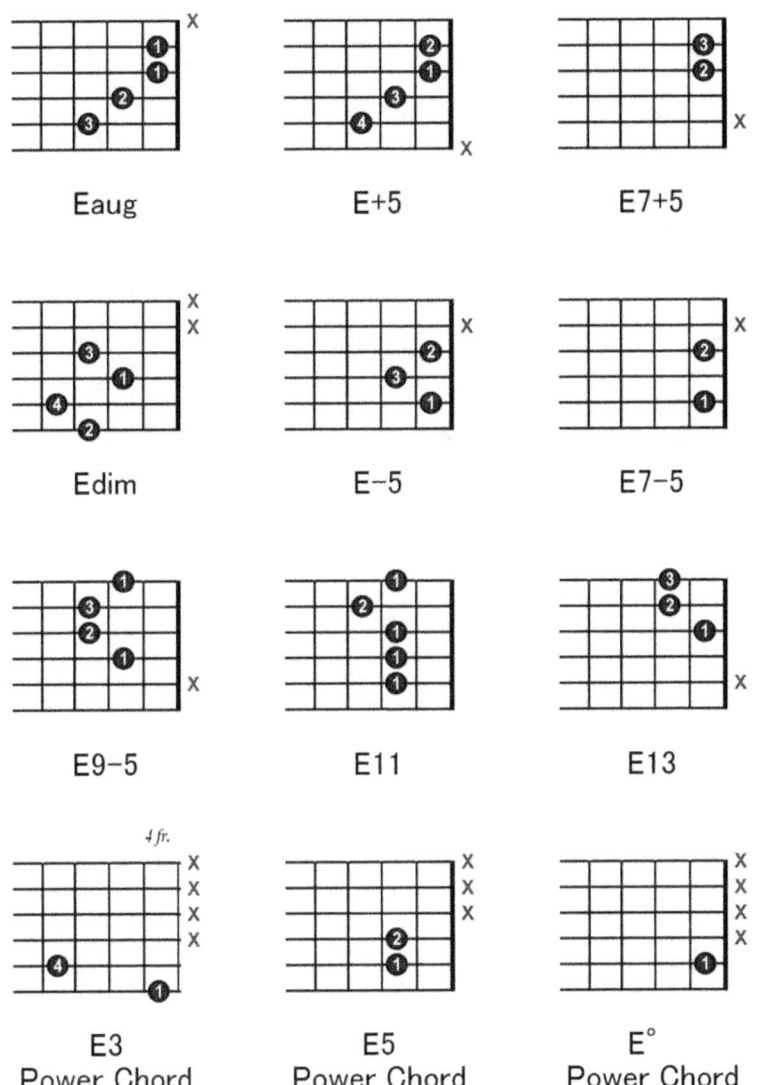

Eaug

E+5

E7+5

Edim

E−5

E7−5

E9−5

E11

E13

4 fr.

E3
Power Chord

E5
Power Chord

E°
Power Chord

F

Chords

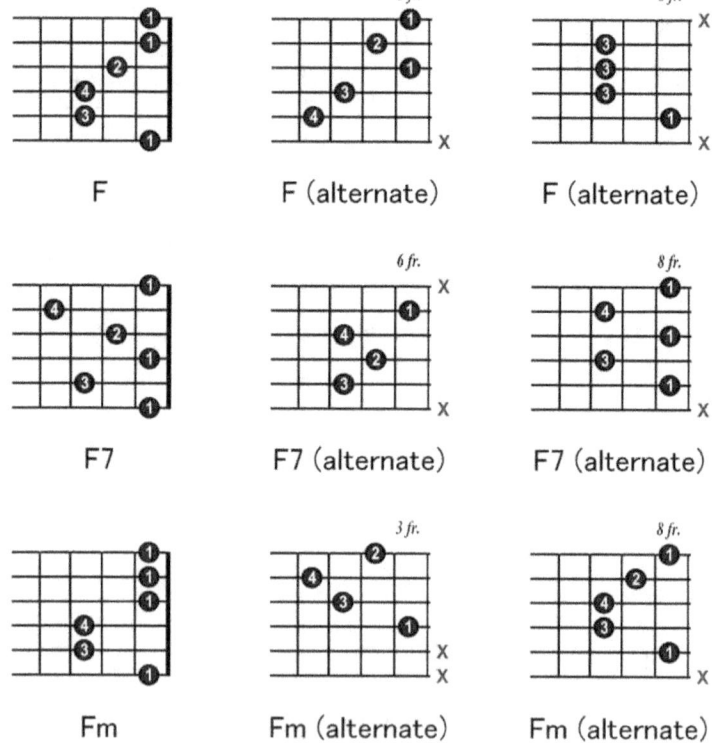

F

F (alternate)

F (alternate)

F7

F7 (alternate)

F7 (alternate)

Fm

Fm (alternate)

Fm (alternate)

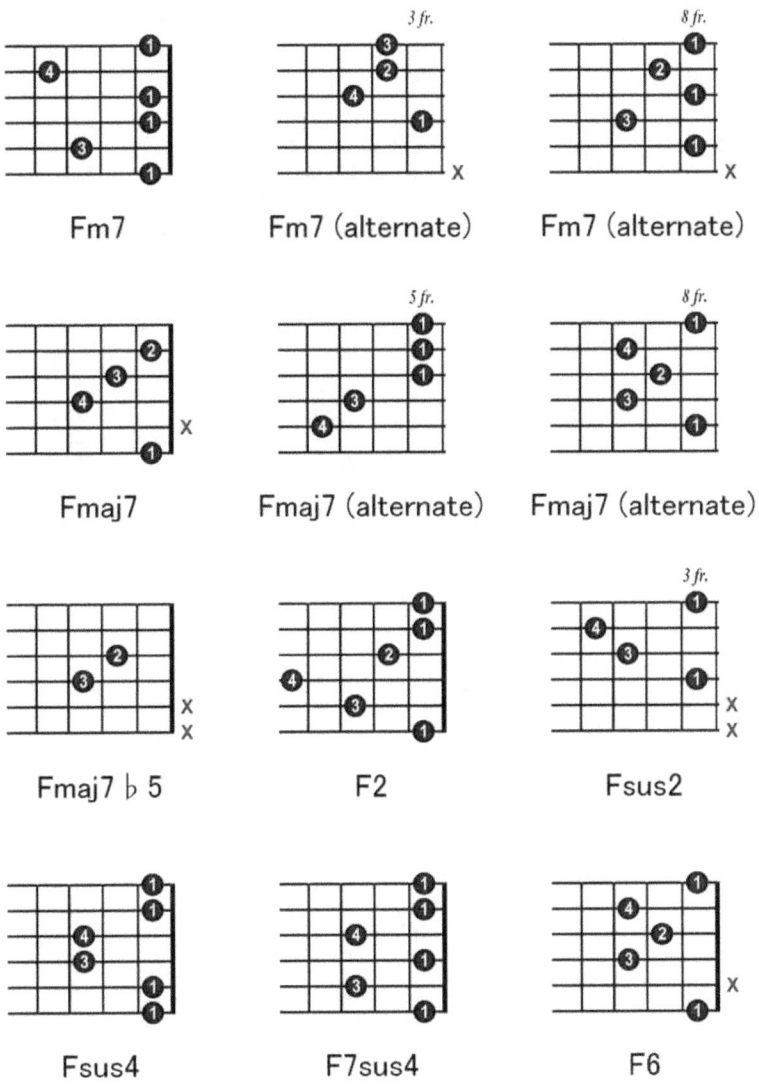

F

Continued

Chords

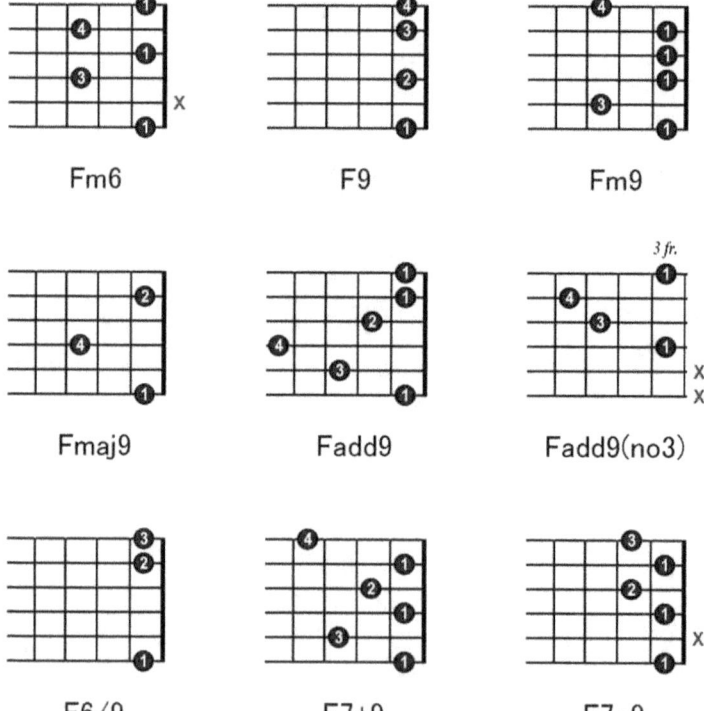

Fm6

F9

Fm9

Fmaj9

Fadd9

3 fr.

Fadd9(no3)

F6/9

F7+9

F7−9

F

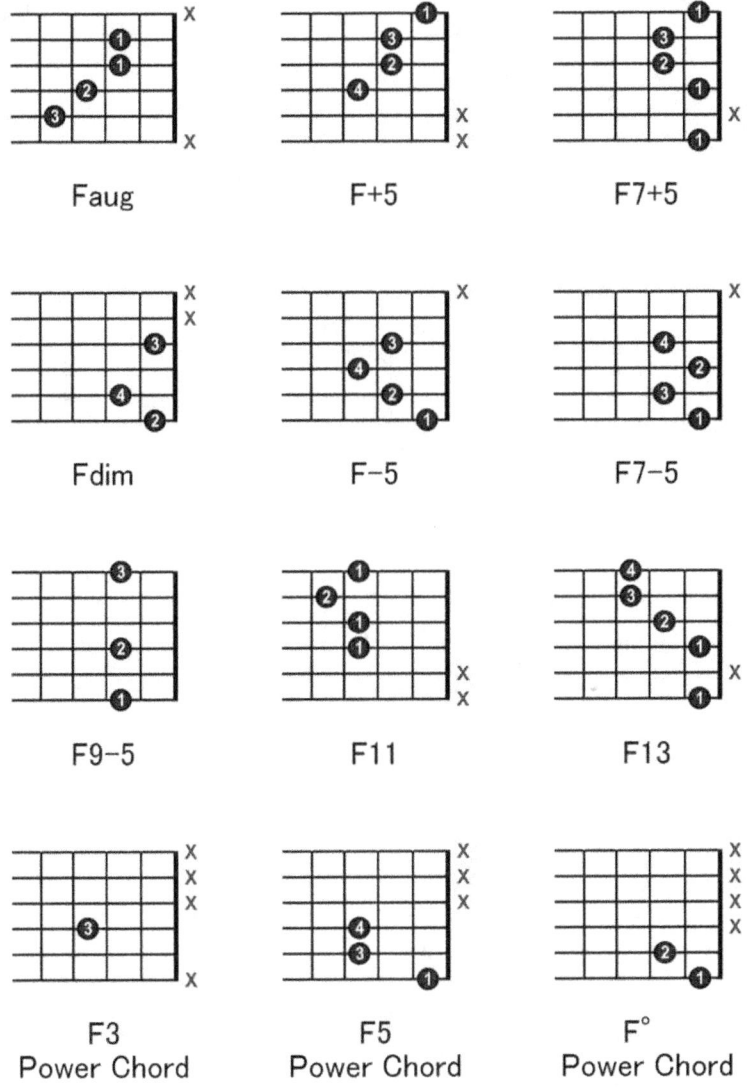

Faug

F+5

F7+5

Fdim

F−5

F7−5

F9−5

F11

F13

F3
Power Chord

F5
Power Chord

F°
Power Chord

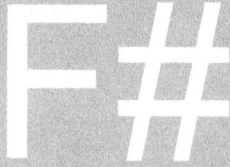

F#

F# is also
known as G♭

Chords

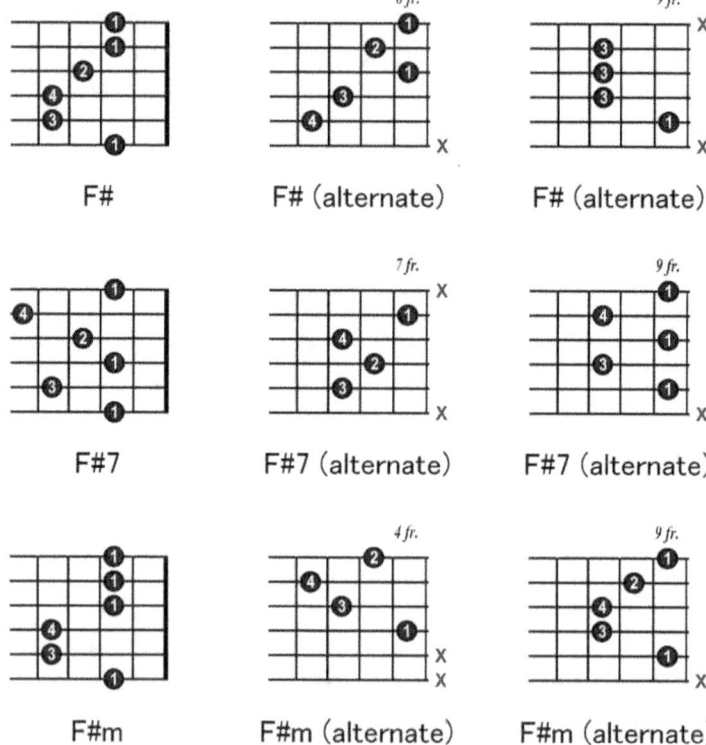

F#

F# (alternate)
6 fr.

F# (alternate)
9 fr.

F#7

F#7 (alternate)
7 fr.

F#7 (alternate)
9 fr.

F#m

F#m (alternate)
4 fr.

F#m (alternate)
9 fr.

Big Left Handed Guitar Chord Book
©2012 Moran Education http://www.MoranEducation.com/6Strings

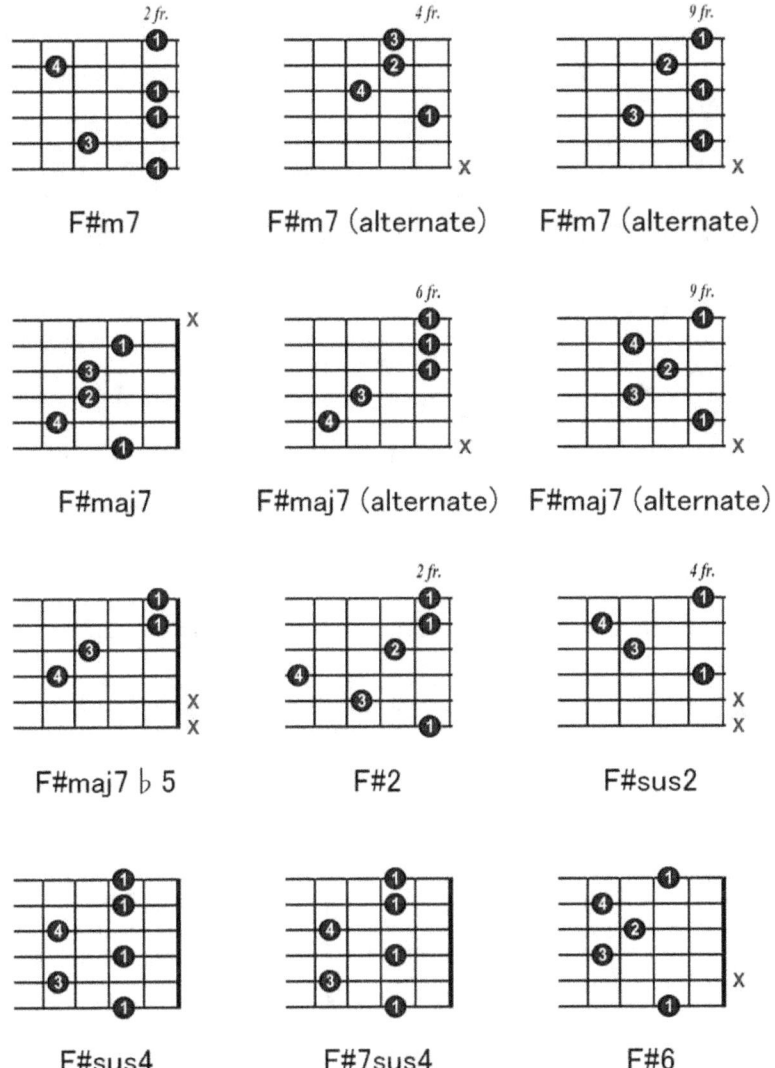

F#m7   F#m7 (alternate)   F#m7 (alternate)

F#maj7   F#maj7 (alternate)   F#maj7 (alternate)

F#maj7 ♭ 5   F#2   F#sus2

F#sus4   F#7sus4   F#6

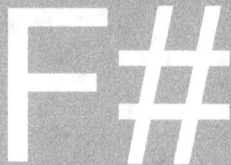

F#

Chords

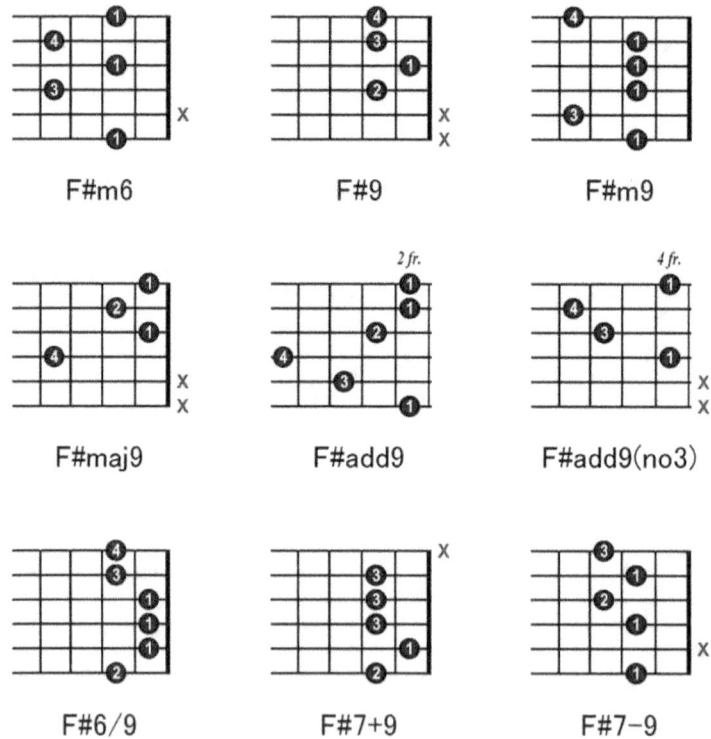

F#m6	F#9	F#m9

F#maj9	F#add9	F#add9(no3)

F#6/9	F#7+9	F#7−9

F#

48

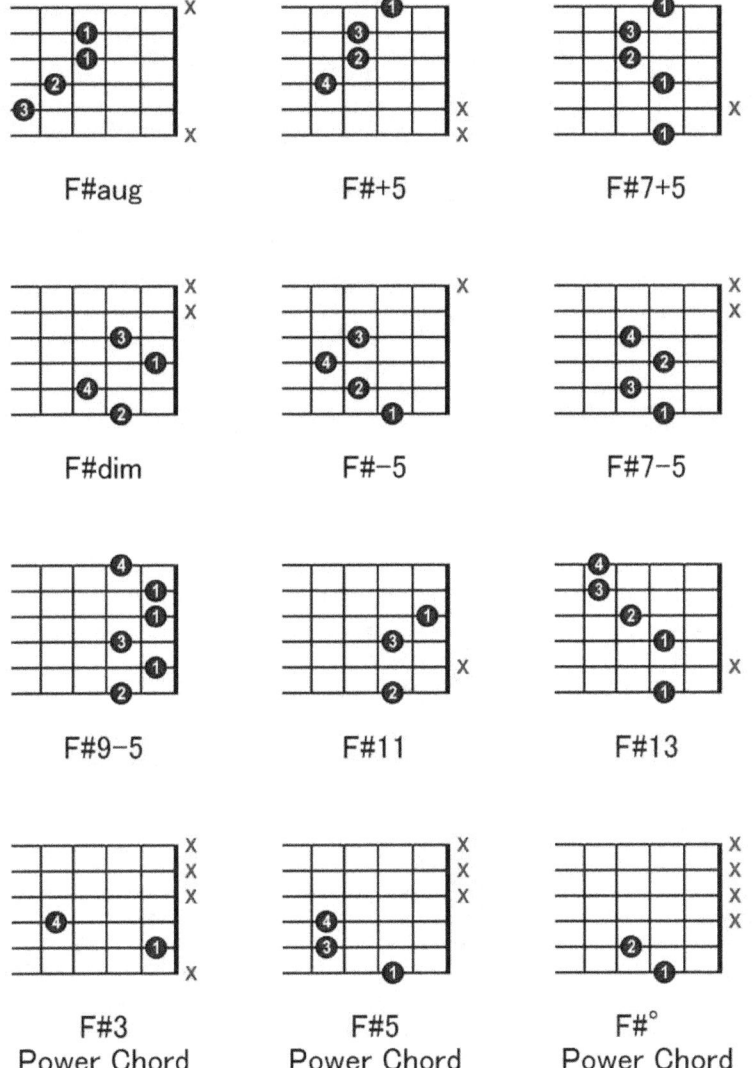

F#aug

F#+5

F#7+5

F#dim

F#-5

F#7-5

F#9-5

F#11

F#13

F#3
Power Chord

F#5
Power Chord

F#°
Power Chord

G
Chords

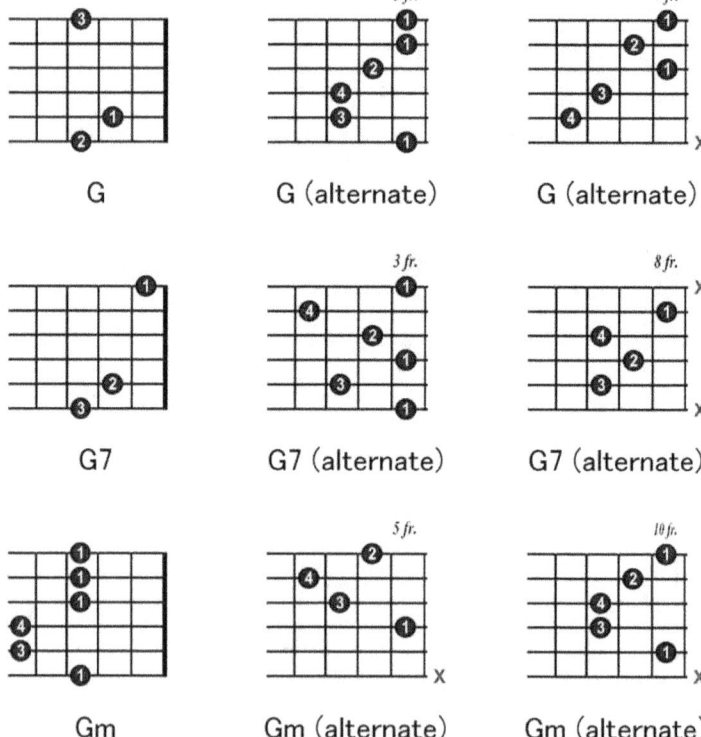

G

G (alternate) *3 fr.*

G (alternate) *7 fr.*

G7

G7 (alternate) *3 fr.*

G7 (alternate) *8 fr.*

Gm

Gm (alternate) *5 fr.*

Gm (alternate) *10 fr.*

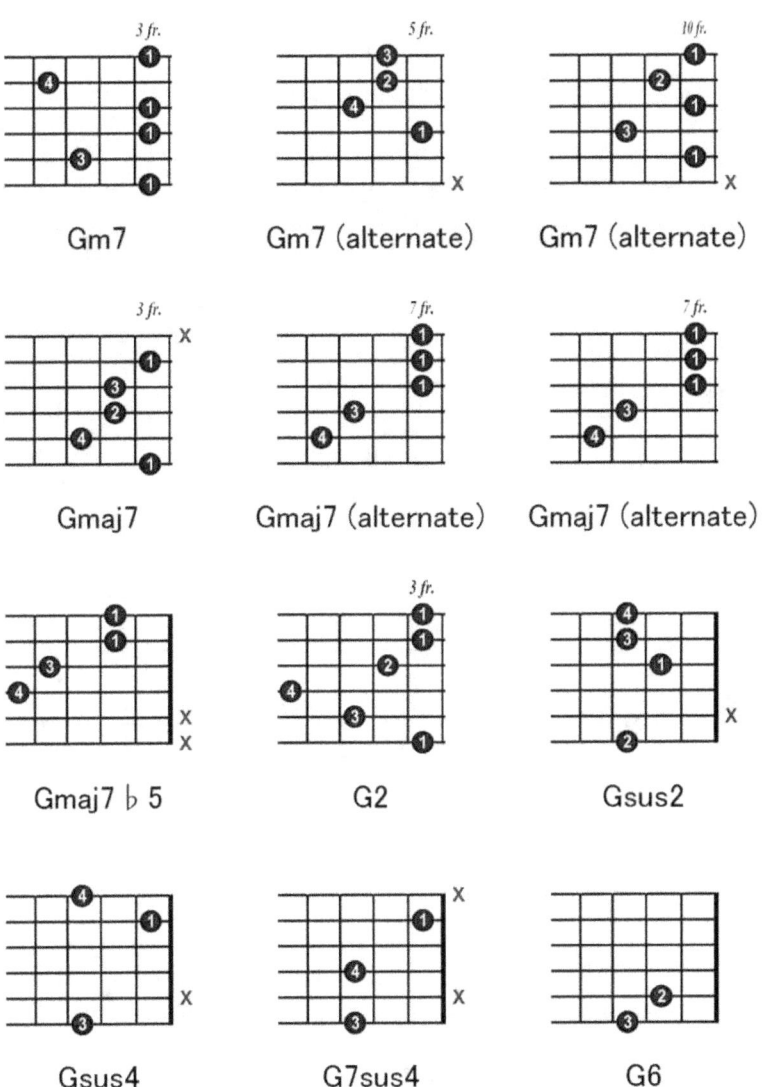

Gm7 Gm7 (alternate) Gm7 (alternate)

Gmaj7 Gmaj7 (alternate) Gmaj7 (alternate)

Gmaj7 ♭ 5 G2 Gsus2

Gsus4 G7sus4 G6

G

Chords

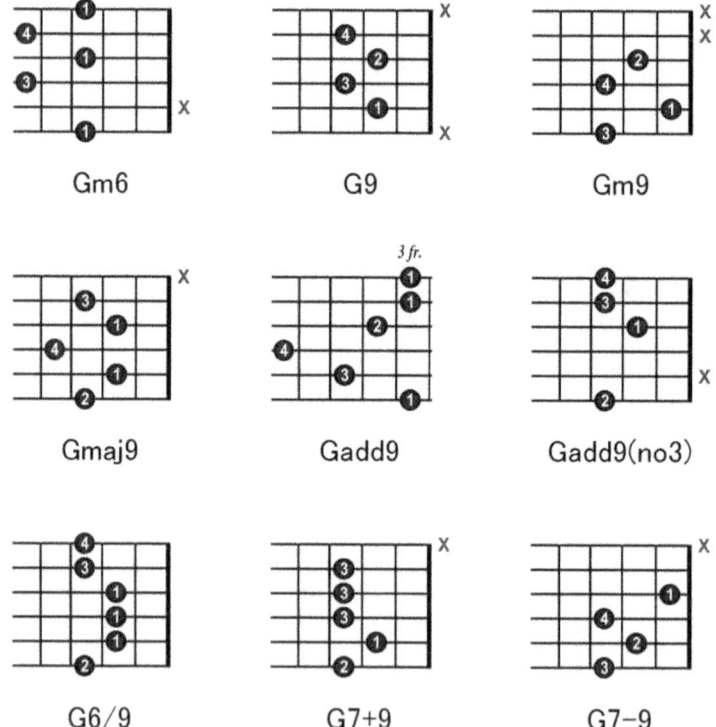

Gm6	G9	Gm9
Gmaj9	Gadd9	Gadd9(no3)
G6/9	G7+9	G7−9

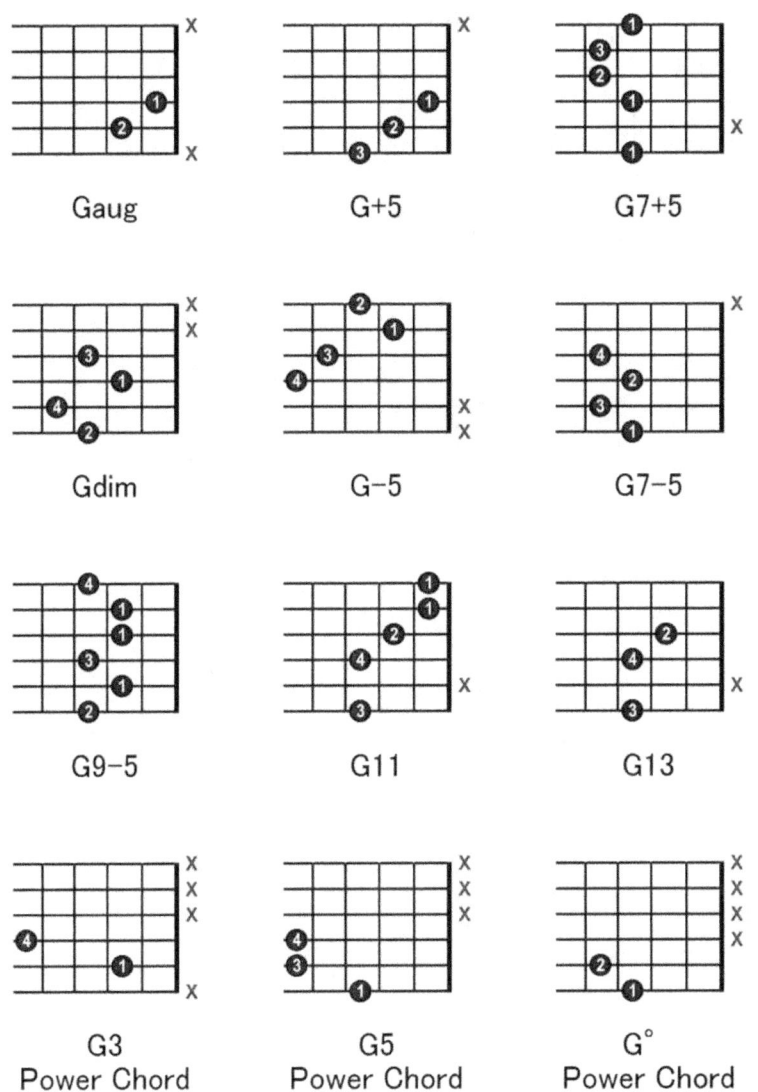

Gaug   G+5   G7+5

Gdim   G−5   G7−5

G9−5   G11   G13

G3
Power Chord   G5
Power Chord   G°
Power Chord

Index | *Find Stuff*

Section	Page No.
Introduction	2
A ♭ Chords	6
A Chords	10
B ♭ Chords	14
B Chords	18
C Chords	22
C# Chords	26
D Chords	30
E ♭ Chords	34
E Chords	38
F Chords	42
F# Chords	46
G Chords	50

6 Strings

View more products in our range, and download free resources for left and right handed guitarists at our website.

www.MoranEducation.com/6Strings

Moran Education

6 Strings - Big Left Handed Guitar Chord Book

Edition I

www.MoranEducation.com/6Strings

ISBN 978-1-4716-5376-6